MISSION
DRIVEN

Moving from
Profit to Purpose

Laura
Gassner
Otting

elevate

Editorial Content: AnnaMarie McHargue
Cover Designer: Arthur Cherry

© 2015 by Laura Gassner Otting

Published by Elevate Publishing, Boise, ID

Printed in the United States of America

ISBN: 978-1937498627
April 2015
07 08 09 10 9 8 7 6 5 4 3 2 1

Library of Congress Cataloging-in-Publication Data

DEDICATION

This book is dedicated to Eli J. Segal, who taught me that
increasing the bottom line means nothing if you aren't also
building a better world, and to Arnie Miller, without whom,
I would never have started this journey.

ADVANCED PRAISE FOR *MISSION DRIVEN*

"*Mission Driven* is that rare find—a book filled with both inspiration and practical advice. Laura Gassner Otting offers an invaluable perspective from her work in executive searches to all those considering a move from success in the world of business to the wide-open world of making a difference."

—**Marguerite W. Kondracke,**
Former President and CEO of America's Promise
Founder, Bright Horizons Family Solutions

"*Mission Driven* is an essential guide for anyone seeking to redirect their talent and energy to build a better world."

—**David Bornstein, Author**
How to Change the World: Social Entrepreneurs and the Power of New Ideas

"I've learned that most social problems can be solved. The question is simply, will enough of our society's most talented, committed individuals channel their energy in the direction of solving them? For the sake of our neediest communities and our society at large, I hope millions of people will find this book. *Mission Driven* is a wonderful resource for everyone from those just getting started in the nonprofit sector to those well along the path."

—**Wendy Kopp, President and Founder of Teach for America**

"If you are looking for a more fulfilling career, *Mission Driven* is the book for you. Laura Gassner Otting combines a wonderfully comprehensive overview of the nonprofit sector with inspiring stories and a step-by-step toolkit that will make your new career a reality. This book covers it all in one very readable, insightful and enjoyable package. Go for it and good luck!"

— **Alan Khazei, Co-Founder and Former CEO, City Year**
Founder and CEO, Be the Change, Inc.

"The phenomenon of the baby boom generation turning 60 provides America with new assets in the form of unprecedented human capital. Laura Gassner Otting will help you catalyze a lifetime of experience and learning into a deeply meaningful second, third or fourth career."

—**Marc Freedman, CEO of Encore.org**
Author, *Prime Time: How Baby-Boomers Will Revolutionize Retirement*
and *Transform America*

"Laura Gassner Otting has created the perfect compass for anyone who has ever considered taking a journey towards work that is fulfilling and makes a difference in the world. Make sure you take *Mission Driven* with you as you walk the path towards your true calling!"

—**Michelle Nunn, Former CEO of the Points of Light Network**

"*Mission Driven* is a great book for any readers who want to combine their skills and their passions through work in the nonprofit sector. The book is an excellent guide to how the 21st century will see a blossoming of nonprofit jobs that are as exciting and demanding as those in the private sector—and even more fulfilling."

—Kathy Buskin, Executive Vice President and COO,
United Nations Foundation
Former President and CEO of the AOL Time Warner Foundation
Former Senior Vice President and Chief Communications Officer at America Online

"Many people have the motivation and skill to work in the nonprofit sector, but don't have the knowledge or confidence to transition into a nonprofit job. This book is a wonderful introduction to career opportunities and considerations in the rapidly expanding nonprofit arena. *Mission Driven* is part instructional guide and part inspirational coach. It offers a practical overview of the nonprofit sector and shows you how you can join in important work that gives back to others."

—Lawrence S. Bacow, Former President, Tufts University

"Individuals 'bridging' thoughtfully from business to the nonprofit sector can be of tremendous value to the organizations and causes they serve, and benefit greatly as well. *Mission Driven* will be a welcome resource for those considering making the transition to mission-focused work."

—David L. Simms, Global Chief Development Officer and President,
Opportunity International
Former Managing Partner of Bridgespan Consulting Group

"In *Mission Driven*, Laura Gassner Otting shares her hard earned wisdom regarding the not-for-profit world. Her engaging style captures the reader's imagination with pithy descriptions of nonprofit organizations and insightful biographical sketches of nonprofit managers. Charitably inclined readers will benefit greatly from Laura Gassner Otting's comprehensive framework for evaluating careers in the non profit world."

—David Swensen, Chief Investment Officer, Yale University
Adjunct Professor, Yale School of Management

"Nonprofits can't do great things without great talent. Laura Gassner Otting inspires you to think broadly about the change you wish to make in the world and provides the tools to make it happen."

—Linda Babcock, James M. Walton Professor of Economics
H. John Heinz III School of Public Policy and Management,
Carnegie Mellon University
and Co-Author of *Women Don't Ask: Negotiation and the Gender Divide*

TABLE OF CONTENTS

INTRODUCTION

In my executive search practice I regularly am asked the following questions by individuals looking to transition from the corporate to the nonprofit sector:

- Is now the right time for me to transition into the nonprofit sector?
- What do I want to do, and where do I want to do it?
- Will my skills transfer to mission-driven work?
- What is working in the nonprofit sector really like?
- How do I deal with the financial ramifications of a nonprofit salary?
- Where do I even begin?

I wrote *Mission Driven*, and the companion text, *The Mission Driven Handbook*, to answer all of those questions and more.

The nonprofit sector is burgeoning with opportunities for career changers. Students are graduating from colleges and universities with bachelor's or master's degrees in nonprofit management. Midcareer professionals are looking around for a better work-life balance in careers that matter to them. Retiring Baby Boomers are finding that they are not so retiring after all. And the nonprofit sector is changing to accommodate the enormous richness of experience all of these individuals can bring with them. These books endeavor to help each of them find their place in the new nonprofit sector.

Mission Driven helps you assess whether the nonprofit sector is right for you and where in this vast sector you can find your place. The accompanying text, *The Mission Driven Handbook*, explores the finer details of how you should conduct your search, with specific tips and tools to enable you to network effectively, write a better résumé, craft more enticing cover letters, and interview as though you've been in the sector for ages. The handbook also includes a compendium of helpful resources, including job-posting websites, education programs, and knowledge tools.

Throughout these books, you will meet others who have made this transition before you. Many of them describe their transition as the best decision they ever made. You will, too.

Welcome to the nonprofit sector! We're glad you are here.

Laura Gassner Otting
Nonprofit Professionals Advisory Group
November 2006
Updated September 2014

CHAPTER ONE:
Is a Nonprofit Career the Right Move for You?

"I enjoy my job, but what really drives me is the volunteer work I do on the weekends . . . I wish I had more time for that."

"I've finally reached my financial goals, but I know that I have one or two more big jobs in me…and I want them to matter."

"I am returning full-time into the workforce… As much as I need a job, I want one that makes a difference."

"I just realized one day: I want more."

If any of these sound familiar to you, it might be the right time to consider a new professional path, following your purpose for a mission driven career in the nonprofit sector.

From every walk of life, at every age, and from every professional background, employees in the nonprofit sector wake up each morning to promising, fulfilling, and demanding careers, working for issues in which they deeply believe or on behalf of causes they truly love. Some have spent their entire careers in the nonprofit sector. Some, like you, considered the change in midcareer. No longer satisfied just to increase the bottom line, they also want to build a better world. They have moved from profit to purpose.

While the transition from the corporate sector to the nonprofit sector may seen natural, logical, or even easy in theory, many career changers find that it is quite tricky in practice. Some find themselves flummoxed by foreign lingo, unfamiliar yardsticks of success, or drastic differences in the pace of the work, while others are simply overwhelmed by the sector's vastness and mission-driven culture. However, with a little assistance in their transition, most find the move into the nonprofit sector to be one of their best life decisions and have wondered, as will you, why they didn't do it sooner.

The desire to make a change in your life—and in your local community or the larger world—will outweigh any difficulties you may face along the way. It will become the overall driving force behind your transition, but going into it with eyes open is still important. This book aims to do just that—open your eyes—helping you to explore the answers to your questions in more detail, providing guides to which type of nonprofit will be right for you at this time in your life and your career, and giving you tools to make this change a reality.

Transitioning into the Nonprofit Sector

The nonprofit sector is experiencing an influx of corporate career changers. Their personal motivations, their chosen pathways, and their challenges and successes may surprise you. The Bridgespan Group, a nonprofit consulting firm that collaborates with social sector leaders to help scale impact, build leadership, advance philanthropic effectiveness, and accelerate learning, performed a 2006 study of sector transition, and their findings are still relevant. Here are some key points to consider from that research:

- More corporate transitioners come to nonprofit work out of a general desire just to *do good* rather than to *do good for a specific cause.*

- Most corporate types found their nonprofit job through personal networking, while others relied on more traditional sources like classified ads or executive search firms.

- Those looking to transition from the corporate sector to the nonprofit sector volunteered at a rate of about twice that of other Americans.

- The quality of people in the sector and the passion they bring to their work are seen as the best aspects of the transition, while financial constraints and the challenges they cause are seen as the worst.

- The nonprofit sector is experiencing growth and turnover, creating opportunities for new talent to drive innovation and change. While some areas of functional expertise transfer better than others, this overwhelming demand for talent opens the window wide for transitioners at every level of nonprofits across the sector.

McKinsey recently surveyed 200 nonprofit CEOs and top managers leading nonprofits, foundations, social enterprises, and impact-investing funds and found consensus around four skills needed to ensure top nonprofit leadership performance:

- Ability to both innovate and implement (58 percent)

- Ability to surround themselves with talented teams (53 percent)

- Ability to be skills collaborators, experienced at bringing multiple stakeholders together (49 percent)

- Ability to manage outcomes and be committed to quality improvements (40 percent)

http://www.mckinsey.com/insights/social_sector/what_social_sector_leaders_ need_to_succeed?cid=other-eml-alt-mip-mck-oth-1411

Explosive Sector Growth = Greater Job Opportunities

Growth in the nonprofit sector has radically outpaced growth in the private and government sectors over the past 30 years. In fact, between 1987 and 2005, the number of nonprofits in the United States grew at nearly triple the rate of the business sector.[1] Even more impressive is that nonprofit sector employment grew 2.6 percent during 2007-2008 (the first year of the recession, when the corporate sector employment shrank 1.1 percent), and grew again 1.2 percent in 2008-2009 (when the corporate sector employment shrank 6.2 percent).[2] As anyone in the corporate sector knows, growth means opportunity. But where does this growth come from, and what does it mean for your career change?

First, the Baby Boomer generation is responsible for creating and leading many of the nation's nonprofits. The mass exodus and leadership deficit predicted by the Bridgespan study met the subprime housing crisis face first, and many of these soon-to-be retirees opted for another tour of duty. The market has strengthened again, however, and the expected rate of nonprofit executive transition will return to the predicted 10 to 15 percent, meaning that three to four out of every five executive director jobs will be vacated during the next three to five years. This will produce a leadership vacuum unparalleled in the history of the nonprofit sector, leaving nonprofits scrambling for experienced managers. More than just causing change at the top, leadership vacuums create ripple effects, sending waves of turnover throughout every level of the organizational chart. In fact, a study by Nonprofit HR Solutions found that 45 percent of nonprofits plan to hire new staff in 2014.[3]

---

1. Independent Sector, "Facts and Figures about Charitable Organizations," (Washington, D.C.: Independent Sector, June 20, 2006 and updated September 20, 2006), *www.independentsector.org/programs/research/Charitable_Fact_Sheet.pdf* (accessed November 26, 2006). Report relies heavily on statistics from the Internal Revenue Service *Data Book,* various editions.

2. Lester M Salamon, S. Wojciech Sokolowski, Stephanie Geller, "Holding the Fort: Nonprofit Employment During a Decade of Turmoil," Johns Hopkins University, Nonprofit Employment Bulletin #39, January 2012.

3. 2014 Nonprofit Employment Practices Survey, Nonprofit HR Solutions http://www.nonprofithr.com/wp-content/uploads/2014/03/2014NEP_SurveyReport-FINAL.pdf (accessed October 22, 2014).

Second, to respond to this leadership deficit, Bridgespan encourages nonprofits to address three difficult but critical imperatives, most of which are also prevalent in the corporate sector:[4]

1. Invest in leadership capacity.

2. Refine management rewards to attract and retain top talent.

3. Expand recruiting horizons and foster individual career mobility.

This is very good news for career changers, particularly the last item. As the staffing needs of nonprofits multiply, hiring corporate employees coming into the sector at all levels will become a common practice. In fact, when I first published this book in 2007, corporate transitioning was still the exception, while now, our firm gets almost weekly inquiries from nonprofits curious—not yet certain, however—about whether hiring from the corporate sector might be the most prudent course of action.

Most nonprofits have neither the historical record of accomplishment nor the current resources to develop top-level senior management from within their own ranks. Further, they often lack the funds necessary to hire top-flight recruiting consultants who scour the Earth for perfect candidates. In fact, only 15 percent of nonprofits have a recruiting budget, and those who do report a median budget of $8,500 per year, hardly enough to even begin.[5] Yet filling this overwhelming leadership vacuum will force the nonprofit sector to take a long, hard look at the types of staff it employs and retains. Nonprofits will need to be much more flexible about the types of candidates they interview and the skills they bring on board. Candidates with experience in rapid-growth environments, expertise in management that is nurturing while still results-driven, and histories of actively grooming internal staff will

---

4. Thomas J. Tierney, "The Nonprofit Sector's Leadership Deficit," (Boston: The Bridgespan Group, March 2006), *www.bridgespangroup.org/kno_articles_leadershipdeficit.html* (accessed November 26, 2006).

5. 2014 Nonprofit Employment Practices Survey, Nonprofit HR Solutions http://www.nonprofithr.com/wp-content/uploads/2014/03/2014NEP_SurveyReport-FINAL.pdf (accessed October 22, 2014).

thrive in the nonprofit sector. This includes, in large part, job seekers from the corporate sector.

Who Transitions into the Nonprofit Sector?

With 13.7 million employees (approximately 10 percent of the country's workforce), it is fair to say that the nonprofit sector employs just about every kind of person you know.[6] People from all walks of life and in different stages of their careers transition into the nonprofit sector. Here are five of the most common types of career changers:

1. *Millennials wanting to get ahead.* Rather than waiting around as the assistant to the assistant to the assistant on an exciting project, young private sector professionals are leaping into the nonprofit sector to get their break. Those in their 20s and 30s are given more opportunities earlier in their careers than they might get in the corporate sector, allowing them to make a splash at a younger age. Whether they leave the corporate world because they are unfulfilled in their day-to-day work, or they are unsatisfied with the overall goal of their nameless, faceless corporation, they usually find the nonprofit sector a breath of fresh, and highly charged, air.

2. *Mid-career professionals looking to gain new skills.* The "generalist professional" nature of the nonprofit sector means that each staffer handles more responsibilities. The nonprofit sector simply does not have the luxury of hiring as many specialists. Therefore, corporate professionals who once were pigeonholed as "just finance," for example, can take on roles in the nonprofit sector that include finance, operations, and administration. Likewise, transitioners who serve on a nonprofit board can use this experience as an opportunity to diversify their background before starting their search. Taking on the program committee chairmanship of a board, for example, is a perfect way to reposition a skill set and a résumé.

---

6. Independent Sector, https://www.independentsector.org/economic_role (accessed October 22, 2014).

3. *Experienced executives looking for work/life balance.* Nonprofits appreciate the whole of a person, not just the small fraction that contributes to increasing shareholder value. New parents enjoy the more family-friendly atmosphere in the nonprofit sector, where they can trade flexible hours for less pay while feeling better about spending time away from their children. Businesspeople who have spent ten years living in airplane clubs in distant airports, too, are thrilled that they can attend soccer games, participate in community activities, and not be exhausted and jet-lagged when it comes to "date night" with their significant others. Nonprofit employees get to contribute to society in their day jobs as well as get encouragement to take time off to pursue other worthy endeavors complementary to the mission of the nonprofit, important to the individual, or, in particularly demanding jobs, their emotional and mental health.

4. *Baby Boomers who are looking to make their final professional chapters about meaning.* According to the Pew Research Center, Baby Boomers are retiring at a rate of almost 10,000 a day,[7] and are increasingly dissatisfied with the direction of our country. For many, newfound free time to travel, play golf, spend quality time with their grandchildren, and volunteer is met with the need to give back, to continue to live a life of purpose, and get back to possible younger and idealistic dreams of changing the world. Seasoned and wiser, they now know that bringing their formidable skills to bear within established nonprofits is a worthy avenue for that energy.

5. *The outraged, the unfulfilled, and the disappointed simply wanting more.* At any and every age, the desire for more out of life encroaches on us all. It's found you, or you wouldn't be holding this book. The nonprofit sector is filled with people from all walks of life—whether they started in the private sector or not—who wanted a

---

7. Pew Social Trends, Pew Research Center, http://www.pewsocialtrends.org/2010/12/20/baby-boomers-approach-65-glumly/ (Accessed October 22, 2014).

more fulfilling professional experience, a way to blend their work with their world, and a road that felt more comfortable for the long haul. These individuals have chosen their nonprofits as the tool by which they are making that change, and the world is richer for having them there.

More Opportunities in Nonprofits

Explosive sector growth has meant a sharp increase in opportunity for those choosing to pursue society's betterment through nonprofit work. During the decade from 2000 to 2010, which includes the worst of the recession, the nonprofit sector saw steady average growth rate of 2.1 percent, while the corporate sector lost jobs at an average rate of -.06 percent. The nonprofit sector grew in nearly every year while the corporate sector contracted and grew and contracted and grew, over and over, in fits and starts. Nonprofit job growth outpaced corporate job growth in every year, and in every region of the country and in every field, except for 2004-2005, where job growth was nearly identical.[8]

Disadvantages and Advantages of Working in the Nonprofit Sector

Just as when working in the corporate sector, you will encounter things in the nonprofit sector that will alternately excite or frustrate you. Some, like fulfilling work and kind coworkers, can be expected. But many, especially increased bureaucracy and burnout, take career changers by surprise. Knowing about both the advantages and disadvantages of nonprofit work *before* you make your move will better prepare you for success. With everything else in the world, there is good news and bad news here. Let's start with the bad news; you'll find it easily trumped by the good.

---

8. Lester M Salamon, S. Wojciech Sokolowski, Stephanie Geller, "Holding the Fort: Nonprofit Employment During a Decade of Turmoil," Johns Hopkins University, Nonprofit Employment Bulletin #39, January 2012.

Disadvantages

Working in a nonprofit can be both fulfilling and maddening at the same time. The industry has its own way of doing things, and insiders know how to navigate the negatives. Here are some of the most common complaints of nonprofit workers.

Concrete Results or Clear Benchmarks of Success Can Be Difficult to Spot

It is often hard to judge the success or failure of daily actions in pursuit of a broader goal. For example, it is easy to know how much a stock price rose, but it is impossible to know that a third grade girl from the inner city went on to become a physicist because she learned about Marie Curie in an after-school mentoring program. Employees in nonprofit organizations sometimes have to "take it on faith" that the work they are doing day to day is contributing to a larger, more important goal.

Work Environments Can Be Frustrating

From antiquated technology to bureaucratic red tape, working in a nonprofit can be downright exasperating. Employees are asked to do more work with fewer resources, create miracles on a daily basis, and satisfy competing interests. The pace of change is often slower than in a corporate environment, given that so many opinions must be considered and the bottom line is not as clear. Personal sensitivities can often impede progress, and predilections and idiosyncrasies must be taken into consideration in any decision. The reward system is as much emotional as monetary, lending itself to pats on the back and inflated job titles. From strategic program direction to the color of the napkins at a fundraiser, few decisions are considered minor in the nonprofit sector.

The Level of Burnout Is High

Those who enter the nonprofit workforce with a specific mission and goal in mind do so with great purpose. This great purpose often places a heavy weight—and even, sometimes, a chip—on the shoulders of those doing the work. Every decision made has deep consequences, and the work is taken extremely seriously. When a worker feels a personal responsibility to the individuals whose lives he is affecting, he is likely to get burned out faster than if he spends his days crunching numbers on a spreadsheet.

The Bottom Line Is Not Always the Bottom Line

Nonprofits base decisions on many important factors, not just the numerical bottom line. In fact, many nonprofits decide to move forward with a program, even though they know it will hemorrhage money. They do this because it is simply "the right thing to do." It may seem like common sense in the corporate world to replace a live person at the front desk with an engraved list of offices and extensions, or to cut down personnel costs by closing the intake office on Saturdays, but to many nonprofits, this sort of personal touch represents their heart and soul.

The Stakes Are Higher

A bad day in your corporate job is unlikely to resemble a bad day in your nonprofit job. Consider the difference between losing a few percent off your stock price and losing a kid to drugs. Consider the difference between closing down a franchise and firing ten employees and closing down a community center that was the lynchpin of a revitalized neighborhood. Compare being told that you can't introduce your products to a new country because they might not be profitable enough and being told that you can't bring immunizations to Africa because of a glitch in U.S. foreign policy. The stakes are simply higher when you are dealing with a cause close to your heart.

There Is a Constant Focus on Fundraising

Nonprofit executives wake up every morning and go to bed every night worrying about the location of their next dollar. This constant pressure leads to certain internal issues going unaddressed until a crisis emerges, takes the chief executive away from the office for long periods of time, and can promote mission drift. Further, most funders prefer to pay for the more tangible costs of program implementation—the actual shots administered to children or meals delivered to elderly shut-ins—and not the far less sexy operating needs—a database, a salary survey, or a desk. Therefore, nonprofits often are forced to ignore vital infrastructure issues until a crisis emerges.

Advantages

Now let's talk about the good stuff, because it is in great abundance and highly rewarding. Whether they are emotional, personal, mental, physical, or spiritual, the advantages of working in the nonprofit sector far outnumber the disadvantages. Perhaps the best advantage, though, is the feeling that it is right for you, right now, to work for something in which you believe deeply and hold close to your heart. With your eyes on the prize, the potentially debilitating disadvantages will fade from deterrents to distractions.

Nonprofits Employ Interesting People

A common misconception is that nonprofits must settle for only those employees willing to work long hours for low pay. On the contrary, nonprofits often get to choose among the best and the brightest candidates and can afford to be picky. As a result, your nonprofit co-workers likely will be exceptionally intelligent, warm, passionate, and caring people, all there because they believe in the mission of the organization. There is something to be said for working with people who have self-selected to work towards a higher goal. While they certainly aren't all saintly, you may enjoy them a bit more than your average corporate coworker.

Unparalleled Growth Opportunities Exist

While three corporate employees may be assigned to one project, one nonprofit employee may be assigned to three projects. Resources are scarcer, so fewer are asked to do more. This leads to faster career development and more varied job responsibilities for those looking to get ahead quickly. Employees in nonprofits can find themselves taking on responsibility for budgets, staffs, and portfolios of larger and more complex work at earlier stages of their careers than their corporate counterparts. In addition, many career changers move back and forth between the sectors, taking advantage of the crash courses obtained in the nonprofit sector each time to achieve more senior positions in the corporate world, only to find themselves ultimately drawn back yet again to the nonprofit sector at an even higher level of responsibility.

Employees Can Shift Skill Sets Quickly

The nonprofit sector loves a generalist. With fewer staff slots than necessary for the work to be done, nonprofits look to employees to multitask and multitask big-time. Therefore, nonprofits offer the opportunity for employees to learn new skills and gain experience in new areas. Those making a career change can use nonprofit experience to shift slowly into a new line of expertise, leaving behind their corporate pigeonhole for a broader nonprofit portfolio.

A Common Vision Makes for a More Compelling Workplace

In the nonprofit you choose, you will find yourself surrounded by co-workers who have made the same decision as you: to work for a cause, this cause in particular. Being surrounded by other "true believers" can be invigorating, energizing, and exciting. Keeping your eyes on the prize becomes easier when it is something you truly value, and getting input and buy-in from co-workers who feel the same way lessens the frustration that comes with late nights and grueling deadlines. In fact, many nonprofit employees are happy to work long hours on a special project for the small price of a few free slices of pizza and a hearty handshake.

The Universe Gets Smaller

Employees at large corporations rarely get to interact with the top brass, either to show their stuff, learn from the best, or simply get reinvigorated on a regular basis. Not so in nonprofits. In fact, because many employees are generalists and organizational structures are often less hierarchical, nonprofit employees can take advantage of a smaller internal community (whether in reality or just in culture). Further, the nonprofit often approaches the external community similarly, not just allowing but actually inviting more junior staff to take part in community-based activities and events, meet community leaders, and broaden their professional and personal horizons.

The Opportunity to Change the World Is Around Every Corner

It used to be that nonprofits universally had seven-year-old computers and insular management thinking. Not anymore. Most nonprofits have become more sophisticated, no longer resembling the dinosaurs of the past, but instead eagerly and nimbly responding to market opportunities. Whether it is a natural disaster half the world away or a donor down the street who wants the organization to "think bigger" about its programs, many nonprofits have employed new thinking, technology advances, and a more entrepreneurial approach to become more agile, adept, and prepared.

There Is Great Innovation in the Nonprofit Sector

Each year, nonprofits are responsible for some of the newest and most exciting thinking around. They look for creative ways to solve the world's most vexing problems, those that were deemed too unprofitable by corporations or too dicey by governments. They bring together public-private partnerships and introduce solutions where none existed before. And they do it while competing for scarce dollars and attention.

Nonprofits Value Business Skills

The nonprofit sector is being flooded with people just like you, who have spent a day, a year, or a whole career in the corporate sector but have decided that now is the time for change. The lines between corporate and community are shrinking, and each sector is rapidly understanding and capitalizing on the value of people from the other. Ten years ago, nonprofits would have looked at a corporate résumé with utter confusion, perhaps even a bit of mirth, but now they see skills and talent that can enable them to accomplish bigger and better things.

Determining if a Nonprofit Career Is Right for You

The nonprofit sector has its own personality and its own quirks. For some, this culture is wonderful; for others, it is downright maddening. Whether or not you fit neatly into one of the categories of transitioners just discussed, or if you are blazing your own path, knowing whether or not the nonprofit sector is right for you demands a critical examination of your personal and career goals, the practical implications of the transition, and your individual motivations.

Questions to Consider

What does this move mean to you on a personal level?

- What change do you want to make in your community, your country, your world?

- If someone gave you $5,000 a month to do whatever you wanted, what would it be?

- Would you rather work for a company or for a cause?

- Would you work harder or longer hours if what you did mattered to you more?

- In what ways are you lacking personal and professional fulfillment in your current work?

- How do you want to give back to the community?

- Do you have a clear sense of how you think the world should be? What would you change?

- Do you want your work to be more personally meaningful?

- Would a job in a nonprofit connect you more deeply to your passion, purpose, or spiritual needs?

- At the end of the day, do you feel that something is missing?

Does a career in the nonprofit sector fit with your personal and career goals?

- What social good would you like to serve, or what change would you like to see in the world?

- How passionately do you feel about this cause? Passionate enough to change your life?

- In what ways would a better work/life balance serve your personal and professional interests?

- What is driving this transition to a nonprofit job?

- Are you running away from your current career or toward a new one?

- Is your current company taking advantage of the full breadth and depth of your skills?

- How would your job satisfaction change if you were working with people more invested in the ultimate outcome of their day-to-day tasks?

- Do you want to work with intelligent and motivated people who are driven by the same mission as you?

- What do you enjoy more, your volunteer work or your regular job? Why?

- What do you want to have done in your career and in your life? What do you want to be remembered for?

What practical impact would a transition into the nonprofit sector have?

- What would be the ramifications of a possible pay cut?

- Would you be satisfied making less money if the work you did was more important to you?

- Why are you looking for a better work-life balance?

- What parts of your current work cause you stress? What would you like to change? What would you like to keep?

- In what ways do you need greater freedom or flexibility in your work environment?

- Is there a place for your skills in the nonprofit sector? Where?

- How much do you need in the way of office resources and staff support to reach your goals?

- Do your family needs, at this time, allow or require that you take this chance?

- What intangible rewards would you want in exchange for, or in addition to, your current career's monetary rewards?

- What time, energy, and resources do you have to develop the skills necessary to be successful in your new nonprofit career?

Reflecting upon Your Answers

Each of your answers, if thoughtfully rendered, reflects your readiness to transition to the nonprofit sector and the direction your job search should take. You may find that you are prepared to start your search today. Or you may realize that your transition is three, five, or ten years away, or even that the nonprofit sector fits more into your after-work volunteer life. Rest assured, there are no wrong answers. Now, let's get started and move you from profit to purpose.

Finding Your Place in the Nonprofit Sector

Now that you have determined that the nonprofit sector is right for you, you must find your place among the sector's many opportunities. Doing so requires a three-tiered decision making process:

1. What is your motivating social cause or problem?

2. What approach would you take to help this cause or solve this problem?

3. What skills and experience to do you bring to the table?

Pinpoint Your Cause

Do you care about saving the whales or teaching children to read? Would you rather fund economic development in villages in sub-Saharan Africa or develop a food bank in your own community? Are you more passionate about creating opportunities for increased access to education or discovering an alternative fuel source?

These are big questions, but your gut and your heart already know the answers. While many people come to the sector wanting generally "to do good," you likely have a preference among the vast number of needy causes.

In Chapter 2, you will learn about the variety of work being done in the nonprofit sector and read about some specific examples of innovative nonprofits. This information may help solidify your choice to work for a cause you know or pique your interest in one that is still unfamiliar.

Determine Your Approach

Nonprofits approach the world's problems in many ways. Consider the problem of the teenage mother. A nonprofit might do direct service, such as running nutritional counseling workshops or prenatal health care. Another nonprofit might advocate on behalf of young mothers, perhaps lobbying state governments for greater food stamp distribution for those purchasing infant formula. Or a nonprofit might raise or distribute money to be used directly by its constituents, such as giving out day care vouchers for high school mothers working towards their GEDs or funding programs that teach mothering skills. Finally, a nonprofit might act as a membership association, gathering together groups of similar individuals for something mutually beneficial, such

17

as pooled health insurance premiums or diaper collections and toy exchanges.

The tactical approach of a nonprofit defines both how it raises and how it spends money. It determines the personalities and skill sets of the employees needed as well. It is reflected in both its mission and its tax status. These implications are described in Chapter 3 in more detail.

Assess Your Skills

Finally, exactly what are you qualified to do? This is where a lot of job seekers fail. They rely solely on how others have defined them in terms of their day jobs but forget to look at the broader picture. You likely have gathered skills at work that are readily inventoried, but what about the rest of the hours in your day? What have you done for your child's school? How have you volunteered in your place of worship? What have you learned along the way through your involvement in neighborhood committees? Have your hobbies or leisure activities lent you expertise relevant to your new career?

Nonprofit job titles tend to be different and may be an amalgam of several jobs you have come to know in the corporate sector. Assessing your skills—from both the paid and unpaid hours in your day—will allow you to see the whole you and enable you to target the right job title for you in the nonprofit sector. Finding the right job will be discussed further in Chapter 3.

Example #1
Jade
Public Relations Executive→Stay-at-Home Mom →
International Teen Health Care Mission Director

Jade spent her corporate career developing public relations campaigns for private, corporate hospitals in Texas. She started her career at large corporations, but after being laid off, struck out on her own. Having had a successful but stressful run, she realized that she missed her young children and wanted to spend more time with them at home and volunteering as a room parent and a fundraiser at their school. She often travels with her children, because raising citizens of the world is important to her.

Jade's children have grown and are now in school all day, and she finds herself at a crossroads. Rather than jumping back into the high-paced world of corporate public relations, Jade now seeks fulfilling work within an interesting organization that values her skills and allows a better work/family balance.

Passions
- ✓ Education
- ✓ Children and family
- ✓ Health care
- ✓ Travel

Tactical Approach
A hands-on person, Jade enjoys developing and implementing actual projects rather than broader, less tangible ideas. She would be more comfortable in an organization that provides direct service. But because of her corporate contacts, she has access to high-net-worth individuals, so she could easily raise money as well.

- ✓ Direct service
- ✓ Philanthropy and fundraising

Qualifications
Jade has a varied background from both her corporate work and individual volunteering.

- ✓ Communications and public relations
- ✓ Fundraising
- ✓ Logistics and coordinating of details, multitasking
- ✓ Start-up and entrepreneurship
- ✓ Substantive knowledge of the health care arena and world travel

Jade might consider becoming an event planner or trip director for a start-up nonprofit that promotes international travel and health care-related humanitarian missions for teenagers, teaching them both the importance of raising funds and an awareness of their place in a responsible society. Her hands-on approach, ability to raise money for travel expenses, knowledge of public relations campaigns to promote trips, and experience with travel and health care enable her to be a real asset to such an organization. Besides, what better way to raise true citizens of the world?

Example #2
Marshall
Corporate Attorney→Social Entrepreneur

Marshall is a patent attorney by training and an outdoorsman by passion. While he has received many accolades for his work at his law firm, he knows that he is only there to pay the bills, biding his time until the weekend comes and he can once again retreat into the woods for a weekend of camping and fishing. He has from time to time taken on some public advocacy work in his community. On his last camping trip, he noticed that a factory, aiming to expand its operations, was encroaching upon his beloved trails. What had once been an annoyance became an all-consuming passion. Once he returned from his trip, Marshall could see nothing but the need to stop this factory in its tracks. His research led him to learn that legions of others are fighting the same war but without the proper battlements.

Passions
- ✓ Environmental protection
- ✓ Sustainable development
- ✓ Access to trails and woods

Tactical Approach

As an attorney, Marshall's first focus is always to work through the courts. He sees solutions in terms of new legislation and increased enforcement. He also understands that once people get out on the trails, they will be unlikely to let such beauty be ruined.

- ✓ Lobbying and advocacy
- ✓ Direct service

Qualifications

Marshall brings experience from his corporate work as well as passion from his weekend camping excursions.

- ✓ Public advocacy
- ✓ Substantive knowledge of the legal system
- ✓ Hands-on knowledge of the effect of corporate encroachment

Marshall might consider becoming an attorney for an environmental defense organization that encourages the active use and protection of public lands. He could use his legal knowledge to wage a campaign in the court system or his advocacy background and personal passion to wage the battle in the court of public opinion. Either way, he's likely to enjoy his day job much more if he's surrounded by people who gather around the water cooler to discuss the great new private camping spot they found, rather than his old crew, concerned only with the latest developments in intellectual property transfer.

Conclusion

Today's nonprofit sector is growing rapidly, and opportunities exist around every corner for making important changes in the world. While the idiosyncrasies of the sector might cause minor annoyances from time to time, the fulfillment and enjoyment you derive from your work will carry the day. The key to success is in finding not just the right sector, but also your personal place in that sector. Learning about the sector as a whole and the roles of its employees will help you to make smart choices that will ease your transition. Now, let's find your next career.

CHAPTER 2:
Overview of the Nonprofit Sector

We all remember the days when our mothers would walk around the neighborhood collecting money for juvenile diabetes or when our fathers would head off in the evenings for their local civic league meetings. We think about soup kitchens and homeless shelters, libraries and schools, or museums and zoos and think we know the nonprofit sector. Think again.

The nonprofit sector today is a dynamic, vibrant, and vast place, filled with every conceivable kind of person and organization and addressing any need you might imagine. Its employees hold Ph.Ds, MBAs, and GEDs and perform work that spans the highly lucrative to the drastically underpaid. The mothers and fathers we remember are still doing their important volunteer work—volunteers are the lifeblood of many nonprofits, after all—but they are now more of an army mobilized to accomplish annual campaigns, not the office staff relied upon for daily support and strategic direction.

Approximately 1.4 million nonprofit organizations are registered with the Internal Revenue Service. Millions more probably exist that are either too small or too informal—those with an annual budget of less than $5,000—to be counted. Public charities (501(c)(3) nonprofits) account for over half of all registered nonprofit organizations and had a combined revenue of $1.51 trillion in 2010. In that same year, over 10.7 million people worked for U.S. nonprofits, representing 10.1 percent of private employment and 9.2 percent of all wages and salaries paid in the United States.[9]

Innovation is the name of the game in nonprofits. Sure, they still serve the tired, the poor, the huddled masses yearning to breathe free, but today's nonprofits no longer resemble the organizations of yore. In an exceptionally competitive market for scarce fundraising dollars, nonprofits increasingly leverage resources for double or even triple plays. Providing beds to a tired and cold family in the middle of winter is a great and noble endeavor, but teaching the mother or father of that family to bake and run a small but profitable café—then funneling those profits back into the purchase of beds and food to benefit more families—is entirely another. This "triple bottom line"—feeding and housing the poor, job skills training, and earned-income generation—is the emerging trend in the nonprofit sector, and career changers will likely find their easiest transitions in nonprofits that have embraced this approach.

What Is a Nonprofit Organization?

Technically speaking, a nonprofit organization is a nongovernmental entity formed to benefit its members or a specific population or cause. According to the Internal Revenue Service, every exempt charitable organization is classified as either a public charity or a private foundation.[10]

Generally, organizations classified as public charities are churches, hospitals (and qualified medical research organizations affiliated with them), schools, colleges and universities. Public charities have an active program of fundraising and receive contributions from many sources, including the general public, governmental agencies, corporations,

---

9. Internal Revenue Service, "Publication 557: Tax-Exempt Status for Your Organization," revised March 2005, *www.irs.gov/pub/irs-pdf/p557.pdf* (accessed November 26, 2006).

10. National Taxonomy of Exempt Entities classification system, a project of the National Center for Charitable Statistics, housed at the Center on Nonprofits and Philanthropy at the Urban Institute, *http://nccsdataweb.urban.org.*

private foundations or other public charities. They also receive income from the conduct of activities in furtherance of the organization's exempt purposes, and they may actively function in a supporting relationship to one or more existing public charities.

Private foundations, in contrast, typically have a single major source of funding (usually gifts from one family or corporation), and most primarily make grants to other charitable organizations and to individuals, rather than directly operating charitable programs.

By Any Other Name . . .

The nonprofit sector is also known as the not-for-profit sector, the voluntary sector, the charitable sector, the independent sector, the social sector, or the third sector. Internationally, nonprofits are called nongovernmental organizations (NGOs).

Determining Your Motivating Cause

As discussed in Chapter 1, finding your place in the nonprofit sector means making three important choices: your motivating social cause or societal problem, the approach you would like to take to aid this cause or solve this problem, and the skills and experiences you bring to the table. We will start with a discussion about the vast number of causes you can serve and then move on to the tactical approach you might take. Chapter 3 will cover how your skills and experience might fit into your new nonprofit career.

Let's start with your motivating cause. Most nonprofits fall into ten major categories.[11] As we walk through nine of them—the tenth is a bit of a generic catchall—you will learn about different nonprofits operating within each category, read about some traditional programs that you may recognize, and learn about exciting, cutting-edge work you may not recognize. In this latter type of organization, where new business thinking permeates daily operations, career changers may find the friendliest transitions.

---

11. Urban Institute Center on Nonprofits and Philanthropy, "The Nonprofit Sector in Brief 2014," Table 3.

Arts, Culture, &
the Humanities

Education

Environment
& Animals

Health

Human
Services

International Foreign Affairs
& National Security

Public &
Societal Benefit

Religious
Nonprofits

Mutual Membership
Benefit

Arts, Culture, and the Humanities

Are you interested in history, music, photography, or painting? Do you attend historical reenactments? Do you enjoy cultural performances and exchanges? Are you part of a singing society or community theatrical group? Do you frequent your local museum or planetarium, library, or monuments? If so, you already know a great deal about the arts, culture, and humanities segment of the nonprofit sector. What you may not know is that this segment also includes publishing activities; radio or television broadcasting; film production; discussion groups, forums, panels, and lectures; and nonscientific study and research, as well as organizations supporting all of these arts, cultural, and humanities nonprofits.

While this category may seem large, its revenues account for less than 2 percent of the entire nonprofit field.[12] Further, only 10 percent of U.S. museums have operating budgets in excess of $15 million,[13] meaning that they must be particularly picky about hiring new staff. Still, there are many jobs for businesspeople.

There are finance, operations, and administrative jobs throughout the nonprofit sector. However, corporate transitioners might take advantage of a new trend in the arts, culture, and humanities sector. Major cultural production nonprofits, like the Metropolitan Opera or the Houston Ballet, are increasingly dividing the leadership post in two, placing all artistic decision-making responsibilities with an artistic director and all business decision-making responsibilities with a business director. Further, these nonprofits also do a brisk business in merchandise, tickets, and reproduction rights, so each organization encompasses revenue-generating models that are perfect for business minds to run.

---

12. American Alliance of Museums, January 2014: http://www.aam-us.org/resources/assessment-programs/accreditation/statistics.

13. Urban Institute Center on Nonprofits and Philanthropy, "The Nonprofit Sector in Brief 2014," Table 3.

Arts, Culture, & the Humanities

Education

Environment & Animals

Health

Human Services

International Foreign Affairs, & National Security

Public & Societal Benefit

Religious Nonprofits

Mutual-Membership Benefit

The arts, culture, and humanities category of the non-profit sector includes the following interests:

- **Arts and culture.** Organizations that promote cultural awareness, folk arts, or arts education; also arts and humanities councils

- **Media and communications.** Film and video, television, printing and publishing, Internet, and radio

- **Visual arts.** Painting, drawing, and photography

- **Museums.** Art museums, children's museums, historical centers, natural history museums, private homes, and science and technology museums

- **Performing arts.** Performing arts centers and all the art that they present, from ballet to opera to musical theater, as well as performing arts schools

- **Humanities.** Organizations that archive or promote the study of history, literature, philosophy, folklore, historic preservation, archaeology, jurisprudence, or comparative religion

- **Historical organizations.** Societies or other groups that support commemorative events

- **Arts services.** Theater education, financial management support, or networking opportunities

Let's take a look at a few arts, culture, and humanities nonprofits.

National Geographic. Yes, that's right. National Geographic is a nonprofit, and it has been for more than a hundred years. From the beginning, National Geographic was created to inspire people to have a lifelong appreciation for the planet and its people, and that mission hasn't changed one bit. National Geographic supports its mission through dues from more than 9 million members and revenues from the sale of its products, all of which align with its mission. While it could assert that the sales of these products create nontaxable revenue, given their mission-supporting nature, National Geographic chooses to pay taxes on this piece of its business to ensure the most flexibility with the revenue.

http://www.nationalgeographic.com

WaterFire Providence. WaterFire is an independent, nonprofit arts organization whose mission is to inspire the 371-year-old city of Providence and its visitors by revitalizing the urban experience, fostering community engagement and creatively transforming a city on the upswing. To do this, they light more than 80 bonfires each year, up and down the center of the river that cuts throughout the city, and gondoliers have toured more than ten million visitors since 1997, bringing the once blighted downtown to life.

http://www.waterfire.org

Contemporary Arts Center. Museums aren't just hushed hallways of stuffy artifacts. In fact, the Contemporary Arts Center (CAC) in Cincinnati is just the opposite. For more than 75 years, the CAC has been a forum for progressive art ideas; it is one of the oldest, most active, and most adventuresome museums of contemporary art in the United States. Founded in 1939 as the Modern Art Society by three visionary local women, the CAC was one of the first institutions in the United States dedicated to exhibiting contemporary art. Always groundbreaking, the CAC became one of the first American institutions to exhibit Picasso's Guernica (1937) and has continued this pioneering tradition by featuring the work of hundreds of now-famous artists early in their careers, including Andy Warhol, Jasper Johns, Robert Rauschenberg, Nam June Paik, I.M. Pei, and Laurie Anderson. In 1990, the CAC pushed the envelope even farther, throwing itself into the center of an important First Amendment legal case, when it successfully defended the right of Cincinnati's citizens to view an exhibition of the photographs of Robert Mapplethorpe.

http://contemporaryartscenter.org

Education

Do you want to promote access to education across diversity and disabilities, build better programming or richer cultural understanding in the classroom, or support faculty and administrators? Have you developed an expertise you would like to teach to a particular population? Education, one of the largest parts of the nonprofit world, might be for you.

Composing about 17 percent of the nonprofit sector,[14] the field of education includes schools, colleges, and trade schools; special schools for the disabled; nursery schools; faculty groups; alumni associations; parent or parent-teachers associations; fraternities or sororities; student societies; school or college athletic associations; scholarships, student loans, and other aid; student housing activities; and foreign exchange programs. Transitioning into this segment may be as easy as transferring your skill set into a supporting administrative role, or it may require additional coursework to gain the required licensure for a hands-on experience.

Contrary to popular opinion, the education sector is not filled with educators. In fact, there are more non-teachers than teachers in the field. Opportunities exist for administrators, student life coordinators, counselors, and entrepreneurs. The charter school movement alone houses a great deal of innovative, start-up thinking. Indeed, some of the most interesting work being done in education today is performed by people from the corporate sector, including school start-ups, endowment management, town-gown relations, or teacher recruitment and retention.

Let's look at some education nonprofits.

uAspire. uAspire works to ensure that all young people have the financial information and resources necessary to find an affordable path to—and through—a postsecondary education. By partnering with high schools, community organizations, and colleges, uAspire counselors

---

14. Urban Institute Center on Nonprofits and Philanthropy, "The Nonprofit Sector in Brief 2014," Table 3.

Arts, Culture, & the Humanities

Education

Environment & Animals

Health

Human Services

International Foreign Affairs & National Security

Public & Societal Benefit

Religious Nonprofits

Mutual-Membership Benefit

The education component of the nonprofit sector includes:

- **Elementary and secondary education.** Preschools, primary and elementary schools, secondary and high schools, special education, and charter schools

- **Vocational and technical schools**

- **Higher education.** Two-year and four-year colleges and universities

- **Graduate and professional schools**

- **Adult education.** Continuing education, certification, and licensing

- **Libraries.** These may be found in communities, schools, foundations, and other public access areas.

- **Student services.** Scholarships and student aid, student sororities and fraternities, and alumni associations

- **Educational services.** Remedial reading and encouragement; parent-teachers groups

have provided college affordability advice to more than 10,000 young people and their families every year. Through their work, college-ready students have found the support and knowledge they need to overcome financial barriers and succeed in college.

http://www.uaspire.org

Building Excellent Schools. To some, charter schools hold the promise of changing public education for our most underserved children. While some impressive charter schools are beating the trends and producing impressive results, there is, at best, uncertainty and disagreement about the overall ability of charter schools to live up to their lofty promise. Building Excellent Schools (BES) supports the design and start-up of high-performing urban charter schools across the country,

and its schools have consistently achieved sustainable, demonstrable success. At its core is the Building Excellent Schools Fellowship, an intense, year-long, full-time, comprehensive training program that prepares individuals (often from the private sector), organizations, and communities to create academically excellent urban charter schools. During its first year, the BES Fellowship resulted in 11 new charter school openings in Massachusetts alone. In the 2012-2013 school year, 36 BES schools, with 65 campuses among them, enrolled 16,773 students nationwide.
http://buildingexcellentschools.org

Spelman College. Founded in 1881 as the Atlanta Baptist Female Seminary, Spelman was incorporated in its current iteration in 1924 and is now a global leader in the education of women of African descent. With 2,100 students from more than 41 states and 15 foreign countries, Spelman has become a breeding ground for women leaders looking to transform themselves, their careers, and their communities through a first class intellectual, creative, ethical, and leadership development platform. With a 80-plus percent graduation rate—one of the best in the nation—there are ample opportunities both within the university and throughout its robust alumni affairs network.
http://www.spelman.edu

Environment and Animals

Are you worried about the state of the planet you are leaving to your children? Do you enjoy the exercise and the environmental benefits of riding your bike to work? Are you concerned about the ever-shrinking planet and the ever-enlarging hole in the ozone layer? Do you leap for joy at the first sign of spring, a telltale sign that you will soon be up to your elbows in new seedlings? Did the stories of pets lost during Hurricanes Katrina and Sandy bring tears to your eyes? You may want to consider a career in the environment and animals segment of the nonprofit sector.

These nonprofits support the traditional conservation and beautification efforts and animal shelters you may remember from

31

Arts, Culture, & the Humanities
Education
Environment & Animals
Health
Human Services
International Foreign Affairs, & National Security
Public & Societal Benefit
Religious Nonprofits
Mutual-Membership Benefit

Environment and Animals

The environmental segment of the nonprofit sector includes:

- **Pollution abatement and control.** Recycling education and support

- **Natural resources conservation and protection.** Land, water, energy, and forest resources conservation

- **Botanical, horticultural, and landscape services.** Botanical gardens, arboretums, and garden clubs

- **Environmental beautification**

- **Environmental education**

The animals component of the nonprofit sector includes:

- **Animal protection and welfare.** Societies to prevent cruelty to animals

- **Wildlife preservation and protection.** Endangered species protection, bird sanctuaries, fisheries, and wildlife sanctuaries

- **Veterinary services**

- **Zoos and aquariums**

your youth, including the preservation of natural resources, combating or preventing of pollution, and animal safety programs. But they also incorporate advanced science and partner with big business to ensure sustainable development, land acquisition for preservation, soil and water conservation, and wildlife sanctuaries or refuges. So, too, have local communities gotten in on the act, with local garden clubs and community garden plots flourishing nationwide. Let's also not forget farming, farm bureaus, agricultural and horticultural groups, and cooperatives, a major piece of this sector.

The environmental movement is perhaps the subdivision of the nonprofit sector least recognizable from its previous incarnations. This field is no longer filled only with hemp-clad hippies who chain themselves to trees and rally against the corporate sector as the last of the great, true evils—though they certainly still exist, and we can thank them for building the sector into what it is today. In fact, the environmental segment of the nonprofit sector now relies on data-driven research, advanced marketing tools, and highly trained advocates. Those from the corporate sector can find themselves at home leveraging public-private partnerships to make new discoveries about energy conservation, creating community investment in public land beautification, or even packaging education models for national distribution in schools.

Animals, too, are big business. Whether in managing the revenue-generating division of an aquarium, developing and marketing tourism packages for wildlife sanctuaries, or implementing a capital campaign to build a new monkey house, those with corporate backgrounds can find many opportunities.

Following are a few examples of nonprofits in the environment and animals sector.

Islandwood. Having grown from a pilot program serving ten Seattle schools, Islandwood is now a national recognized organization rooted in an integrated approach to scientific learning about our environment, self-awareness about our role within it, and stewardship of it for generations to come. Located on 255 acres on beautiful Bainbridge Island, as well as many off-site locations, Islandwood is an ideal learning environment for children and adults alike who seek to discover a new way of seeing nature, themselves, and one another, and in doing so, how to change the world for the better.
http://www.islandwood.org

The White Dog Cafe Foundation. Over the last 30 years, the White Dog Cafe of Philadelphia has become a model enterprise, known nationally for its community involvement, environmental stewardship, and responsible business practices. Its foundation, established in 2002, creates, strengthens, and connects locally owned businesses and farms that are committed to working in harmony with natural systems; providing meaningful, living-wage jobs; and supporting healthy community life. It supports this mission with two programs. The Sustainable Business Network of Greater Philadelphia is a network of local business people, professionals, social entrepreneurs, investors, nonprofit leaders, and government representatives who are committed to building a more socially, environmentally, and financially sustainable local economy. Fair Food builds wholesale markets for local farmers; improves distribution channels for locally grown food; increases consumer access to local food grown with care for people, animals, and the Earth; educates people about the value of locally and sustainably raised food; and increases the supply of humanely and naturally raised animal products in the Philadelphia marketplace.

http://www.whitedog.com

The Bronx Zoo. As the number-one family attraction in New York City, with more than 4 million visitors per year, the Bronx Zoo and its related parks and zoos has a golden opportunity in its hands. The Wildlife Conservation Society, headquartered at the Bronx Zoo, has capitalized on this, taking the smartest branding and marketing thinking from the corporate world and plunking it right in the middle of the lions and tigers and bears . . . oh my. Its highly successful corporate partnership program allows corporations to do anything from sponsoring a fun-filled family weekend at one of the five parks (Bronx Zoo, New York Aquarium, Central Park Zoo, Prospect Park Zoo, and Queens Zoo) to supporting educational and conservation programs around the world. With companies like Pepsi, Hess, Fisher-Price, Bank of America, Delta Airlines, Wendy's, ConEdison, and Norwegian Cruise Lines as customers, the Bronx Zoo has certainly become king of the sponsorship jungle.

http://www.bronxzoo.com

Health

Do you loyally stand in line once a quarter to donate blood, race out and gather medical supplies for every natural disaster, or run in your local 10K for cancer each year (or just wish you did)? Have you ever spent time translating overly technically insurance forms for a friend or colleague, wondering why it has to be so difficult for a sick person to access the care they need? Are you a steadfast believer that, with enough time and resources, we can find a cure to most anything that ails us? If you believe in the power of a healthy universe and want to do anything you can to make it a reality, a job in the massive health sector of the nonprofit world may be for you.

Generating almost 60 percent of the revenue of all nonprofits,[15] the health segment is certainly the largest segment in the nonprofit sector. This doesn't mean that your neighborhood primary care clinic has any money; it just means that the nonprofit research giant down the street has lots more. Typically seen as hospitals, nursing homes, and public health clinics, these kinds of nonprofits also include rural medical facilities, blood banks, rescue and emergency services, visiting nurses, aid to the handicapped, pharmaceutical supplies, scientific research for cures to diseases, health insurance and group health plans, community health planning, and mental health care. Below, the sector is discussed in its three largest breakout subsectors: health care; mental health and crisis intervention; and diseases, disorders, and medical disciplines.

Health Care

Have you often wondered why those with less money get worse health care treatment? Are you frustrated by the legions of poor who are forced to seek general care in the emergency room? Do you want to find solutions that open the doors of health care for all, regardless of socioeconomic status, language barriers, or education? If so, transitioning from a direct service or administrative position in a corporate setting into one in the nonprofit sector may be right for you.

15. Urban Institute Center on Nonprofits and Philanthropy, "The Nonprofit Sector in Brief 2014," Table 3.

Many nonprofit health care providers, such as hospitals, operate in a manner similar to that of their corporate counterparts. The major difference is that the revenues of the nonprofit are reinvested in the organization in the form of fee reductions, educational programs, and community outreach. Also, health care nonprofits tend to focus on preventative health measures, such as family planning or public education.

Let's look at a couple of health care nonprofits.

VisionSpring. VisionSpring was established by the partners of Scojo Vision, LLC, which donates 5 percent of its profits to the foundation. VisionSpring trains local women entrepreneurs (because studies show that when women have access to their own capital, they use it to feed, educate, house, and provide medical care for their children) to give basic eye exams and sell low-cost reading glasses in their communities.

Health Care

The health care component of the nonprofit sector includes:

- **Hospitals.** Community health systems, general hospitals, and specialty hospitals

- **Ambulatory and primary health care.** Group health practices and community clinics

- **Reproductive health care and family planning**

- **Rehabilitative care**

- **Health support.** Blood banks, emergency medical services and transportation, and organ and tissue banks

- **Public health**

- **Health support and financing**

- **Nursing facilities and health home facilities**

By providing people with the tools to see, VisionSpring improves their health and extends their working life by 50 percent. At the same time, they help raise the standard of living for local entrepreneurs and their families.

http://visionspring.org

PlayPumps International. Picture a playground in rural Africa filled with laughter. Now imagine that a merry-go-round in that playground, filled with spinning children, is powering a pump a few feet away that brings water to the entire village. It's a simple yet innovative idea. PlayPumps International, a nonprofit based in the United States and Africa, has installed over 1,000 PlayPumps in South Africa so far and aims to install thousands more, bringing clean water to 10 million people in the next three years and eliminating some of the more 2.2 million deaths caused by water-related illnesses per year.

http://www.playpumps.co.za

Mental Health and Crisis Intervention

Have you or someone you loved suffered because of mental illness? Have you seen the terrible effects of families torn apart because of a lack of support in a crisis? Do you approach all people with great empathy and understanding, believing that everyone can succeed if only given a chance to compete on equal footing? If so, you may find a career in a mental health or crisis intervention setting quite rewarding.

Like the health care segment of the nonprofit sector, organizations that deal with mental health and crisis intervention can offer smooth transitions for direct service providers and administrators from the corporate world.

Below are a couple of nonprofits that work with mental health and crisis interventions.

National Domestic Violence Hotline. In 1994, then Senator Joseph R. Biden and Senator Orrin G. Hatch coauthored historic legislation, the Violence Against Women Act, and Congress responded to the nation's

Mental Health and Crisis Intervention

The mental health component of the nonprofit sector includes:

- **Substance abuse dependency, prevention, and treatment**

- **Mental health treatment.** Psychiatric hospitals and community and residential mental health centers

- **Hot lines and crisis intervention.** Domestic violence and depression help

- **Addictive disorders.** Eating disorders, smoking disorders, or gambling additions

- **Counseling services.** Either in one-on-one or group settings

- **Mental health disorders and associations**

high rate of domestic violence by enacting the legislation and creating the National Domestic Violence Hotline (NDVH), an independent nonprofit. Since then, the Hotline has become the vital link to safety for over 1.5 million families, responding to more than 16,000 calls each month. NDVH serves as the only domestic violence hotline in the nation with access to more than 5,000 shelters and domestic violence programs across the United States, Puerto Rico, and the U.S. Virgin Islands. The Hotline is toll-free, confidential, and anonymous and operates 24 hours a day, 365 days a year. Help is offered in more than 140 different languages through interpreter services, and a TTY line available for the deaf, deaf-blind, and hard of hearing.
http://www.thehotline.org

Screening for Mental Health. Screening for Mental Health, Inc. (SMH) first introduced the concept of large-scale mental health screenings with its flagship program, National Depression Screening Day, in 1991. SMH programs now include both in-person and online programs for depression, bipolar disorder, generalized anxiety disorder, posttraumatic stress disorder, eating disorders, alcohol problems, and suicide prevention. SMH's programs have been used by hospitals, mental health centers, social service agencies, government agencies, older adult facilities, primary care clinicians, colleges, high schools, corporations and HMOs, reaching individuals from teens to older adults. SMH's programs have reduced the stigma that inhibits many individuals from seeking treatment and have helped people to identify mental illness and specific ways to access treatment for themselves or a loved one.

http://mentalhealthscreening.org

Diseases, Disorders, and Medical Disciplines and Supporting Research Organizations

Have you lost a loved one to a disease that could have been prevented or should have been cured long ago? Are you appalled by news of a disease that has obliterated whole populations of unsuspecting children? Are you convinced that we are "this close" to finding cures to diseases that our grandchildren will never have to fear? If so, and even if you have no particular medical training, look no further than the medical and research segment of the nonprofit sector.

Diseases are cured through research, and research is expensive. Those with experience as a medical practitioner will transfer easily into this field, like a teacher in the education subsector, relying on their interest in contributing to a greater purpose and their medical expertise. Those without a medical background can contribute through fundraising, operations, marketing, and public affairs, as well as lobbying campaigns, which facilitate efficient operations and garner increased attention and funding from domestic and international governments.

Certainly you've heard of the multiple nonprofits organized around specific diseases, like multiple sclerosis, breast cancer, or HIV/AIDS. Let's look at other organizations in this segment that support both the victims of disease and cures through research.

Diseases, Disorders, and Medical Disciplines

The diseases, disorders, and medical disciplines and research segment of the nonprofit sector addresses the following issues:

- Birth defects and genetic diseases
- Cancer
- Diseases of specific organs
- Nerve, muscle, and bone diseases
- Allergy-related diseases
- Digestive diseases and disorders
- Specifically named diseases
- Medical disciplines
- Research around any of these areas

PATH. What if products and strategies meant to improve health in the developing world were designed expressly for the people who need them? Instead of tossing expensive answers at problems unique to poor countries, PATH's mission is to find and create effective, sustainable solutions that work best where they're needed most. These include health technologies that are appropriate for use in remote villages, immunization programs built side-by-side with the governments that administer them, and cultural projects that spark dialogue and social changes in communities at risk from HIV.

The results are staggering: hundreds of thousands of women in Afghanistan, Ghana, and Mali are receiving PATH-developed tetanus toxoid vaccine; thousands of youth in Cambodia, Kenya, Nicaragua, and Vietnam access reproductive health services from pharmacy staff who have received training through PATH's programs and curricula;

nearly a half-million individuals at high risk for HIV have received one-on-one information and counseling from 4,300 PATH-trained community workers in the Philippines; and thousands of girls in Kenya have participated in a PATH-sponsored rite-of-passage program that provides an alternative to female genital mutilation.

http://www.path.org

Partners In Health. As never before, the world is focused on averting millions of preventable deaths in the developing world and is throwing substantial funding at the problem. Yet for this massive investment to make a real impact on the twin epidemics of poverty and disease, a comprehensive, community-based approach is key. Partners In Health's (PIH) success has helped prove that allegedly "untreatable" health problems can be addressed effectively, even in poor settings. Until recently, conventional wisdom held that neither multidrug-resistant tuberculosis (MDR TB) nor AIDS could be treated in such settings. PIH proved otherwise, developing a model of community-based care, which was used successfully to treat MDR TB in the slums of Lima, Peru, and to deliver antiretroviral therapy for AIDS in a squatter settlement in rural Haiti. Today, elements of PIH's community-based model of care have been adapted by other countries and programs throughout the world.

http://www.pih.org

Shop Well with You. Serving as a body-image resource for women surviving cancer, their caregivers, and health care providers, Shop Well with You (SWY) was founded by a 25-year-old woman who watched her own mother's struggle through four bouts of breast and thyroid cancer. While cancer often alters a woman's body image or self-perception, SWY helps each woman move beyond being identified primarily by her cancer to being recognized by her other attributes—a mother, friend, wife, sister, daughter, mentor, artist, advocate, and so on. Through its website, SWY focuses on helping women improve their self-image and quality of life by giving them customized clothing tips arranged

41

Arts, Culture & the Humanities

Education

Environment & Animals

Health

Human Services

International Foreign Affairs & National Security

Public & Societal Benefit

Religious Nonprofits

Mutual Membership Benefit

by cancer-related treatments and side effects, compiled in a resource kit tailored to the client's size, financial resources, fashion preferences, and medical condition.

http://shopwellwithyou.org

Human Services

In each and every city, local nonprofits exist to better the community for all. You've likely been asked for money for one of these, or read about a contentious not-in-my-back-yard (NIMBY) debate occurring between community members and local and state elected officials. If you have ever worked for the benefit of those in your neighborhood, wanted to become more invested in your community, or desired to create social justice for all (even those actually in your backyard), this may be the segment for you.

Human services nonprofits may focus on low-income and moderate-income housing, elderly housing and housing for the disabled, area economic development or renewal, homeowners' associations, business redevelopment, community promotion, or loans or grants for minority or woman-owned businesses. They also may help assist and support local safety officers in crime prevention or voluntary firefighter's organizations. In some communities, these nonprofits may include community chests, booster clubs, or other grant-making organizations.

Crime and Legal-Related Services

Do you have a law degree sitting around gathering dust, either because you never used it or never used it in the way you once had hoped? Those pesky student loans pushed many an aspiring public interest attorney into more lucrative corporate work, where the golden handcuffs proved harder to unlock than originally expected. Perhaps you have been touched by the stories of death row pardons after new evidence came to light? Or maybe you have seen ex-offenders contributing to society after paying their debt and want to find ways to facilitate re-entry into society? If so, consider looking into one of the many crime, crime-prevention, and legal-related nonprofits.

Crime and Legal-Related Services

The crime and legal-related component of the nonprofit sector includes:

- **Crime prevention.** Youth violence and drunk driving prevention

- **Correctional facilities.** Halfway houses for offenders and ex-offenders

- **Rehabilitation services for offenders.** Prison alternatives and inmate support

- **Administration of justice.** Mediation and dispute resolution

- **Law enforcement.** Community policing

- **Protection against abuse.** Spousal, child, and sexual abuse prevention

- **Legal services.** Public interest law

The legal field has, perhaps, the largest historical track record of pro bono work. Many nonprofit leaders have long used lawyers and legal professionals who work full-time in corporate endeavors. They already know the value that a lawyer from the private sector can bring and is able to readily envision your transition. For the job seeker, developing nonprofit experience will be relatively easy through providing hands-on assistance or creating programs that are implemented by others.

Let's look a closer look at one legal-related organization.

Fresh Lifelines for Youth (FLY). Fresh Lifelines for Youth (FLY) is an award-winning nonprofit dedicated to breaking the cycle of violence, crime, and incarceration of teens. Through a unique and powerful combination of programs—legal education, leadership training, and one-on-one mentoring—FLY helps more than 2,000 youth in Santa

Clara and San Mateo's juvenile justice system, or those "at-risk" of entering the system, get off probation, engaged in school, and back on track with their lives.

http://flyprogram.org

Employment & Workforce Development

Imagine a job seeker looking to start over, reaching into a new career in a new industry for a second chance to do something more. Sound familiar? Many people are attempting to start a new career, but criminal records, poor training, missing education, or simply a lack of mentors and role models can be major obstacles. Perhaps you can empathize with their plight? If so, working with nonprofits focused on employment preparation, procurement, rehabilitation, or security may be of interest to you.

Whether it's workforce development, welfare-to-work partnerships, or skills training for youth, nonprofits that enable advances in employment provide a plethora of opportunities for those looking to move into the nonprofit sector. Individuals with human resources, training and development, or counseling experience will find that their skills have prepared them well for this type of work. The most innovative nonprofits working in this segment combine training, education, and

Employment & Workforce Development

The employment component of the nonprofit sector includes:

- **Employment preparation and procurement.** Vocational counseling and job training

- **Vocational rehabilitation.** Goodwill Industries; sheltered employment

- **Labor unions**

safety nets with an intense understanding of community, client, and customer needs and emerging labor trends.

We'll look at a couple of organizations that prepare people for employment.

Citizen Schools. Since 1995, Citizen Schools has built a creative, effective learning model that addresses community needs while building student skills through hands-on experiential learning activities. Citizen Schools operates a national network of apprenticeship programs for youth that connects middle school students with adult volunteers in hands-on learning. At Citizen Schools, students develop the academic and leadership skills they need to do well in school, get into college, and become leaders in their careers and in their communities. Citizen Schools currently enrolls 5,300 middle school students and engages 4,700 volunteers at 32 campuses nationwide, but it envisions a day when most of the nation's 88,000 schools reopen after school, on weekends, and in the summer for experiential learning opportunities that powerfully link children and schools to the larger community. *www.citizenschools.org*

Encore.org. Encore.org is spearheading efforts to engage millions of people spend their vital later years towards the betterment of society. By using the power of personal stories to change the narrative about later life and by creating and supporting pathways to connect interested people (you?) with opportunities for work with societal benefits, Encore.org has begun to redirect "the great gray wave" into work for the common good. *http://www.encore.org*

Food, Agriculture, and Nutrition

Do you get incensed when you see babies with apple juice in their bottles? Are you appalled by the lack of good nutritional choices in schools and see childhood obesity as the next public health epidemic? Do you frequent your local organic farmers' market each week—and buy

Food, Agriculture, and Nutrition

The food, agriculture, and nutrition component of the nonprofit sector includes:

- **Agricultural programs.** Farmland preservation, animal husbandry, and farm bureaus

- **Food programs.** Food banks, congregate meals, soup kitchens, and meals on wheels

- **Nutrition**

- **Home economics**

extra for the family down the street? If so, you may enjoy a nonprofit career in providing more and better food choices around the block and around the world.

Without subject matter expertise, most corporate transitioners come to this segment to manage a food bank or market nutritional programming in school. Others bring a commercial banking background, using their expertise to make microloans to small communities in emerging markets. Much of the exciting work in this area involves combining agricultural needs with the development of third world countries.

Here are two examples of nonprofits working in this space.

W.K. Kellogg Foundation. Some of our country's largest foundations are making significant investments on particular issues. For the W.K. Kellogg Foundation, one of those issues is food safety and security. It is critical to a child's overall health that they grow up with access to good food and opportunities for physical activity. Yet, too many children—and disproportionately those in low-income communities and communities of color—are growing up without either, leading to an escalation of chronic illnesses, reduced life outcomes, and increasing health care costs. The W.K. Kellogg Foundation strives to change this by supporting national and local partners in collaborations that lead to healthy people, healthy farms, healthy communities, and healthy economies. It is just one way a foundation with billions of dollars of assets can leverage national presence, decades of wisdom, and ready access to be a player on the local stage.

http://www.wkkf.org

Heifer International. Today, millions of people who were once hungry will be nourished by milk, eggs, and fresh vegetables. Families who, for generations, knew only poverty are building new homes and starting businesses. Children who once headed out to the fields to do backbreaking work are heading into schoolrooms to learn to read. And people who never thought they'd be in a position to help someone else experience the joy of charitable giving. How is this possible? Because someone has given them a cow, sheep, or pig. It's a simple idea: give an animal to an impoverished family, with the promise that they pass along any offspring of that cow to their neighbors. Through livestock, training, and "passing on the gift," Heifer has helped 20.7 million families and currently works in more than 30 countries around the world, giving people the tools and training they need to sustain their lives.

http://www.heifer.org

Housing and Shelter

Does the thought of a person living in a car make you wish you could do something to help? What about a whole family, without the car, in the dead of winter? Do you have skills in human resources, banking, or mental health counseling, but aren't sure how to help? Do you believe in giving both a handout and a hand up? If so, you will find great rewards in the housing and shelter segment of the nonprofit world.

Some housing and shelter programs are intertwined with community banks, thus offering a natural transition point for many from corporate banking, real estate, or financial services careers. The analytic and assessment skills, and the understanding of community players, enable the corporate career changer to bring along a ready-made tool kit of

Housing and Shelter

The housing and shelter segment includes:

- **Housing development, construction, and management.** Low-income and subsidized rental housing, retirement communities, independent housing for people with disabilities, and housing rehabilitation

- **Housing search assistance**

- **Temporary housing.** Homeless shelters

- **Homeowners' and tenants' associations**

- **Housing support.** Housing improvement or repairs and cost reduction support

transferable skills. Further, many of these nonprofits have created social venture models to underwrite housing costs.

We'll take a closer look at two nonprofits in the housing and shelter segment.

Rubicon Programs. Rubicon was established in 1973 in Richmond, California, by community members concerned about the closure of state psychiatric hospitals. The founders recognized the need to develop local services for people disabled by chronic mental illness who were returning to the community. Although finding solutions for this major social issue was in itself an ambitious job, Rubicon also took on the problems of poverty and homelessness, building and operating affordable housing and providing employment, job training, mental health, and other supportive services to individuals who have disabilities, are homeless, or are otherwise economically disadvantaged. Each year, Rubicon helps over 3,000 people in the San Francisco Bay area. Not your typical nonprofit, Rubicon operates its own social enterprise initiatives that help fund other programs while also employing and training clients.

http://www.rubiconprograms.org

Boston Community Capital. Economic, social, and civic isolation among individuals and communities are barriers to healthy communities, economic independence, and wealth creation. Boston Community Capital recognizes this problem and has created a financial intermediary system that serves low-income and disadvantaged people and communities by connecting them to the mainstream economy through a range of financial vehicles, services, and products and by acting as an investment banker in those communities. This nonprofit works through a loan fund, lending money to organizations and private developers to provide housing, community facilities, and social services for low-income people and neighborhoods. It also works through a venture fund, making equity investments in high-potential, emerging businesses that create a "double bottom line" of financial and social returns, thus strengthening businesses that build healthy communities. *http://www.bostoncommunitycapital.org*

Public Safety, Disaster Preparedness, and Relief

It's been hard to watch the news recently. Images hurtle towards us: babies in the arms of firefighters; grief-stricken mothers carrying dead children; families torn asunder by plague, famine, floods, or terrorism. Each is more horrible than the last. Have these events inspired you, like many, to make the sector switch? Or have you always been driven to help out during disasters? Do you find yourself scrambling to organize clothing, blood, or toy drives? Do you always line up first to support those who support others in times of crisis? Do you feel the best measure of protection is an ounce of prevention? If so, you may belong in a public safety, disaster preparation, or disaster relief nonprofit.

Corporate career transitioners can find a home for themselves at almost any level in these organizations. From project management to crisis intervention to fundraising and operations management, the tactical and strategic thinking honed in MBA programs and in corporate careers make for an ideal employee in this segment. While the nonprofit sector prides itself on valuing the experience of each human being, an

49

> **Public Safety, Disaster, and Relief**
>
> **The public safety, disaster preparedness, and relief segment includes:**
>
> - **Disaster preparedness and relief services.** Search and rescue squads and fire prevention
>
> - **Safety education.** Automobile safety and first aid
>
> - **Public safety benevolent associations**

approach that can rise above calamity and bloodshed is, in fact, highly prized in these positions.

Here are some nonprofits that work in the public safety, disaster, and relief segment.

The American Red Cross. The American Red Cross, a humanitarian organization led by volunteers and guided by its Congressional charter and the seven fundamental principles of the International Red Cross Movement, provides relief to victims of disasters and helps people prevent, prepare for, and respond to emergencies. The American Red Cross functions independently of the government but works closely with government agencies, such as the Federal Emergency Management Agency (FEMA), during times of major crises. The disaster with the highest death toll since the founding of the American Red Cross was the 1900 hurricane in Galveston, Texas, in which an estimated 6,000 people were killed. Clara Barton herself, founder and then president of the American Red Cross, gathered a team and traveled by train from Washington, D.C., to Galveston as soon as she heard news of the disaster. The most expensive disaster was Hurricane Katrina, which necessitated the greatest mobilization of Red Cross workers for a single relief operation.

http://www.redcross.org

i-SAFE, Inc. In this day and age, everyone knows students can, thanks to the Internet, explore the marvels of the world and travel to the most intelligent realms of our galaxy. But many do not know that if students are not cautious, they can become entrapped in the most detestable realms of the human imagination. Concerned people realize that true online safety is not found in software filters but in education and community support. Founded in 1998 and endorsed by the U.S. Congress, i-SAFE is the leader in Internet safety education. Available in all 50 states, Washington, D.C., and Department of Defense schools located across the world, i-SAFE's mission is to educate and empower youth to make their Internet experiences safe and responsible. The goal is to educate students on how to avoid dangerous, inappropriate, or unlawful online behavior. i-SAFE accomplishes this through dynamic K-12 curriculum and community outreach programs involving parents, law enforcement, and community leaders. It is the only Internet safety foundation to combine these elements.

http://www.isafe.org

Recreation and Sports

Do you love the great outdoors but feel stuck inside at work all day? Are you a weekend warrior who counts the days until it's gloriously Saturday once again? Do you look back on your childhood days at camp as some of the most influential and meaningful experiences of your life? Why not combine your passion with your abilities and work in one of the many nonprofits focused on bringing recreation to the masses?

Camps, gyms, and recreation clubs exist in the corporate sector and nonprofit sector alike. Running them is not hugely different in either sector, with the exception of those organizations that cater to specific populations. The nature of their business remains the same. People with consumer-oriented backgrounds and a deep love of activity may enjoy combining their business expertise with a recreational hobby or a cause dear to their heart.

Recreation and Sports

The recreation and sports component of the nonprofit sector includes:

- **Camps**

- **Physical fitness and community recreation facilities.** Parks, playgrounds, and recreation centers

- **Sports associations and training facilities**

- **Recreational clubs**

- **Amateur sports.** Leagues of any sport you can imagine, from badminton to horse jumping

- **Amateur sports competitions**

Following are a couple of nonprofits with recreation or sports missions.

Special Olympics International. If you think that the Olympics are inspiring, try going to the Special Olympics. For over 43 years, with training and competition in 32 Olympic-style sports, Special Olympics athletes have been spreading the message that people with intellectual disabilities can—and will—succeed when given the chance. And, we're not just talking about the handful that Eunice Kennedy Shriver assembled in her backyard as a response to her outrage about unfair and unjust treatment she witnessed in the 1950s. We're talking 4.4 million athletes in 170 countries around the globe.
http://www.specialolympics.org

The Fresh Air Fund. The Fresh Air Fund was created in 1877 with one simple mission—to allow children living in disadvantaged communities to get away from hot, noisy city streets and enjoy free summer vacations in the country. When The Fund began, New York

City was overflowing with poor children living in crowded tenements. Many of these youngsters were hit by a tuberculosis epidemic, and "fresh air" was considered a cure for respiratory ailments. Over the past 125 years, The Fresh Air Fund has provided free summer vacations in the country to more than 1.8 million New York City children from disadvantaged communities. Each year, thousands of children visit volunteer host families throughout the U.S. and Canada through the Friendly Town Program or attend Fresh Air Fund camps.
http://www.freshair.org

Youth Development

Are you a firm believer that children are the future? Do you take extra time to mentor a neighborhood youngster or guide one of your children's peers? Did a mentor, a teacher, or an extracurricular activity once have a life-changing effect on you, so much so that you want to share it with the next generation? If so, think about joining one of the many nonprofits that serve youth. They include those that promote and support scouting, mentoring, tutoring and scholarship, orphanages, prevention of abuse and neglect, juvenile delinquency, camps, extracurricular programming, and agricultural apprenticing.

During the last 15 years, nonprofits facilitating youth service (i.e., youth performing dedicated and demonstrable volunteer work) have

---

Youth Development

The youth development segment of the nonprofit sector includes:

- **Youth centers and clubs**

- **Adult and child matching programs**

- **Scouting organizations**

- **Youth development programs.** These might focus on agricultural, business, citizenship, or religious leadership

---

exploded in number. Some of the best are run by social entrepreneurs, those individuals who walk and talk like an MBA and care and share like a nonprofiteer. Opportunities abound in the youth service and development segment for those with a corporate background to make a real change in the future.

You know some of these organizations from your own childhood: the Girl Scouts, your local YMCA, Big Brothers, Big Sisters, Camp Fire, and 4-H Clubs. Let's take a look at some newer youth-oriented organizations.

City Year. Calling itself an "action tank" for national service, City Year helped found the national and community service movement. It demonstrated, improved, and promoted the concept of national service as a means for building a stronger democracy in 17 cities nationwide and in South Africa. City Year's signature program, the City Year youth service corps (part of the AmeriCorps movement) unites more than 1,000 young adults from diverse backgrounds, ages 17 to 24, for a demanding year of full-time community service, leadership development, and civic engagement. Their subject area focus is on education and serving our nation's most underserved schools. Yet, the bigger picture shows City Year to be a catalyst, engaging people and institutions in the citizen service movement, and leads innovative policy discussions around national service policies and initiatives. Since 1988, City Year has graduated 8,200 corps members, and a recent study found that alumni are more likely to vote and volunteer. City Year's vision is that one day, the most commonly asked question of a young person will be, "Where are you going to do your service year?" *http://www.cityyear.org*

Camp Starfish. When most people think of summer camp, the images that come to mind are of canoeing and soccer, arts and crafts, nature hikes, and care packages filled with candied contraband. They also remember making friends, trying new experiences, and succeeding at things they never thought possible. Come to Camp Starfish, and you'll see the same things: the ubiquitous smiles, the contagious laughter, and the camaraderie that only summertime can bring. But look a little closer, and you'll start noticing that something is a little different. Camp Starfish, founded in 1998, serves at-risk children with emotional, behavioral, and learning problems. With its unique and remarkable one-to-one camper-to-staff ratio, Camp Starfish enables children not only to succeed, but to learn that success is, in fact, an option available to them.

http://www.campstarfish.org

General Human Services

If you are coming to the nonprofit sector because you simply want to help people, but none of the human services causes seem holistic enough, you may be looking for a nonprofit that simply serves populations as a whole. Perhaps you want to help autistic children, teenage mothers, or disabled adults? Maybe you are interested in facilitating adoption or improving the lives of those in foster care facilities? Perhaps you once got trapped in a cycle of debt and, having slowly crawled out, vowed you would assist others who found themselves in a similar predicament? If so, look no further than the many nonprofits that broadly, but ably, serve our wonderful human race with specific tools (like education and access) against broad goals (like poverty alleviation and opportunity for socio-economic mobility).

Human service nonprofits are historically funded in large part by public sources, relying heavily on city, county, state, and federal dollars. Public funding means public scrutiny, and public scrutiny means the books have to be spotless. Corporate transitioners may well find abundant opportunities in finance, administration, and operations roles in these nonprofits.

Following are two examples of human service nonprofits.

SingleStopUSA. Single Stop harnesses America's most effective anti-poverty tools to create economic mobility for low-income families and individuals. Through a unique one-stop shop, Single Stop provides coordinated access to a safety net worth $750 billion and services

Human Services

The human services component of the nonprofit sector includes:

- **Human services.** The Urban League, Salvation Army, Volunteers of America, Young Men's and Young Women's associations, and neighborhood centers

- **Children and youth services.** Adoption, foster care, and child day care

- **Family services.** Single parent agencies, family violence shelters, in-home assistance, family services for adolescent parents, family counseling, and pregnancy centers

- **Personal social services.** Financial counseling and transportation assistance

- **Emergency assistance.** Traveler's aid and victims' services

- **Residential and adult day care programs.** Hospices, supportive housing for older adults, group homes, and adult day care centers

- **Centers to support the independence of specific populations.** Centers that work with seniors; developmentally disabled persons; immigrants; the blind or visually impaired; the deaf and hearing impaired; and lesbian, gay, bisexual and transgendered individuals

provided by 1.5 million nonprofits—connecting people to the resources they need to attain higher education, obtain good jobs, and achieve financial self-sufficiency. Single Stop is on track to connect one million households in eight states to $3 billion of resources and services. To achieve this, Single Stop provides community-based organizations (CBOs) and community colleges with training, evaluation, program support, change management consulting, and proprietary technology. These tools empower sites to provide low-income families with wraparound services that include benefits screening, application assistance, case management, tax preparation, and legal and financial counseling.

http://www.SingleStopUSA.org

National Urban League. The National Urban League is a historic civil rights organization dedicated to economic empowerment in order to elevate the standard of living in historically underserved urban communities. Founded in 1910 and headquartered in New York City, the National Urban League spearheads the efforts of 95 local affiliates in 300 communities in 35 states through the development of programs, public policy research, and advocacy. In 2014, they launched One Nation, Underemployed, which identified that the major impediments to equality, empowerment and mobility are jobs, education, access to living wage, and wealth parity. Their programs and advocacy efforts focus on raising up the voices and the skills of their 2 million members to harness local resources and influence national policies towards these goals.

http://nul.iamempowered.org

International, Foreign Affairs, and National Security

Did you ever dream about running off and joining the Peace Corps? Have you noticed that while the world has gotten a lot smaller, you feel we do not yet know or respect our neighbors enough? Are you fed up with feeling helpless about foreign atrocities? If so, the international, foreign affairs, and burgeoning national security segment of the nonprofit sector is for you.

These days, businesses large and small operate in a global community. Transitioners who can bring a global focus and understanding to the nonprofit sector can thrive in one of the many international, foreign affairs, or national security nonprofits.

Let's take a closer look at two such organizations with an international focus.

> ### International, Foreign Affairs, and National Security
>
> **The international, foreign affairs, and national security segment includes:**
>
> - **Promotion of international understanding.** Cultural exchanges, academic exchanges, and other international exchanges
>
> - **International development.** Agricultural and economic development, international relief, and the development of democratic or civil societies
>
> - **International peace and security.** Arms control, national security, and United Nations associations
>
> - **International affairs, foreign policy, and globalization.** The development of international economic and trade policy
>
> - **International human rights.** International migration and refugee issues

Trickle Up. Trickle Up is a 26-year-old nonprofit global microenterprise development organization working in Asia, Central America, and West Africa to provide opportunities for the very poorest people to improve their living standards by developing microenterprises via a combination of seed capital grants, training, and support services. Working with a network of partner agencies in five core countries, Trickle Up served 7,558 new participants in 2012, improving the lives of nearly 40,000 people around the world.

http://www.trickleup.org

People to People International. With the notion that "peaceful relations between nations require understanding and mutual respect between individuals," President Dwight D. Eisenhower founded People to People International (PTPI) in 1956. Since it became an independently operated nonprofit in 1961, hundreds of thousands of people—from elementary students to senior citizens—have participated in PTPI Chapter activities, worldwide conferences, adult exchange programs, or student exchange programs. PTPI underwrites its activities through revenue-generating ventures such as cultural exchange trips, clothing sales, conferences, and holiday cards.

http://www.ptpi.org

Public and Societal Benefit

Do you find yourself defending those who cannot defend themselves? Are you constantly pushing the agenda of social justice within your corporation or community? Have you been able to build capacity in your local nonprofit by sharing your business skills as a board member or volunteer? If encouraging nonprofits to expand their reach through increased voluntarism, grant making, leadership development, or mutually beneficial relationships interests you, than consider a career in the public and societal benefit segment.

Civil Rights, Social Action, and Advocacy

Set up either to influence public or political opinion around a population of people long-term (the AARP will never run out of subjects to tackle) or short-term to pass or defeat a certain piece of legislation on the ballot this November, advocacy organizations exist on every conceivable subject. They may focus broadly on getting out the vote, voter registration, or voter education; provide facilities or services to political campaign activities; or support, oppose, or rate political candidates. Or they may spotlight a specific issue, like gun control, abortion, government spending, separation of church and state, school vouchers, nuclear weapon disarmament, labor rights, zoning, capital punishment, ecology and conservation, consumer protection, peace, drug and alcohol abuse, welfare, urban renewal, or pornography.

Those with legal backgrounds can find an abundance of opportunities in civil rights, social action, and advocacy nonprofits. As educational campaigns and lobbying are a huge piece of the advocacy puzzle,

Civil Rights, Social Action, and Advocacy

The civil rights, social action, and advocacy segment includes:

- **Civil rights.** Minority, disabled, women's, seniors', children's, and lesbian and gay rights

- **Intergroup and race relations**

- **Voter education and registration**

- **Civil liberties.** Reproductive rights, right to life, censorship and freedom of speech and press, and right to die/euthanasia

transitioners with public relations and advertising expertise can also find a place.

We'll look at a couple of nonprofits in the civil rights, social action, and advocacy segment.

Campaign for Tobacco-Free Kids. Tobacco use killed 100 million people in the 20th century. If the current trends continue, tobacco will kill one billion people in the 21st century. Every day, 80,000 to 100,000 young people around the world become addicted to tobacco, statistics that when followed to their ultimate conclusion mean that 250 million children and young people will die from tobacco-related diseases. The Campaign for Tobacco-Free Kids envisions a world where these statistics don't exist, and through their advocacy work in the United States and all over the world, they have been beginning to change laws that govern affordability, access, and understanding. And, oh yeah, remember the 1998 settlement where Big Tobacco paid billions to cover just some of the cost of the harm their product created? You can thank CTFK for their major role in that fight.

http://www.tobaccofreekids.org

Citizen University. Citizen University runs a conference each year where hundreds of change makers, activists, and catalysts meet in Seattle to learn about power, build their networks, and recharge their sense of purpose. They come from all states across the country, points on the political spectrum, and a wide range of missions—from immigrant rights to national service, voting reform to veteran re-integration, civic education to Hollywood and technology. Together they talk about ways that citizens can solve problems in new ways, bypassing broken institutions, stale ideologies, and polarized politics. Together they are working to rekindle citizenship in America by training citizen leaders of today and tomorrow.

http://www.citizenuniversity.us

Community Improvement and Capacity Building

Do you regularly join local civic league or community service projects? Do you believe that change begins in your own backyard? Are you frustrated by the way nonprofits are managed and want to find ways to increase their knowledge, ability, and skills needed to fulfill their important missions? Do you enjoy teaching others the skills you have gained in the corporate sector but want to do it in an environment where the end result is social change rather than just an increase in shareholder value? Are you a proponent of compulsory national and community service for high school graduation, or would you like to see voluntary community service as an option with benefits similar to the G.I. Bill? Take a look at the community improvement and capacity-building segment.

Community involvement and capacity-building nonprofits are likely homes for people with a background in business. Partnerships have long been formed between nonprofits and the communities in which they work; their boards include corporate community members, and they fundraise from local professionals. Nonprofits benefit from consultative support around a specific problem, like strategic planning, fund development, or an earned income business launch.

Arts, Culture & the Humanities

Education

Environment & Animals

Health

Human Services

International Foreign Affairs, & National Security

Public & Societal Benefit

Religious Nonprofits

Mutual-Membership Benefit

Community Improvement and Capacity-building

The community improvement and capacity-building segment includes:

- **Community and neighborhood development.** Community coalitions and neighborhood and block associations

- **Economic development.** Urban, community, and rural development

- **Business and industry.** Chambers of commerce, real estate associations, or boards of trade

- **Nonprofit management.** Nonprofit development and support

- **Community service clubs.** Rotary, Knights of Columbus, or 100 Black Men

Let's look at a few community improvement and capacity-building nonprofits.

First Book National Book Bank. The First Book National Book Bank provides new books to children from low-income families across the country, using generous donations from children's book publishers, service donors, and volunteers. By making large-scale donations to the First Book National Book Bank, publishing companies save the cost of multiple book shipments to fulfill donation requests and can refer organizations requesting book donations to First Book. In addition, First Book integrates donations into cause-based marketing campaigns and creative, large-scale media and marketing efforts that serve the promotional goals of publishing companies. Thanks to generous donations of book surpluses from its publishing partners and assistance in distribution from the U.S. Coast Guard, the First Book National Book Bank reaches programs in every corner of the country, serving national and local nonprofit organizations and serving the broad spectrum of children in need.

http://firstbook.org

Taproot Foundation. As you well know, barriers exist between business and the nonprofit sector, and these barriers lead to a squandering of talent available to both sectors. The Taproot Foundation harnesses human capital by connecting millions of business professionals in the United States with nonprofits who need their talents and experience. Through pro bono service partnerships, the Taproot Foundation helps nonprofits develop critical infrastructure, redefines volunteering for businesspeople, and fosters an ethic of service across professional fields. Since 2001, over 7,500 Taproot Foundation volunteers have given 1.5 million hours of pro bono consulting valued in excess of $140 million.

http://www.taprootfoundation.org

Philanthropy, Voluntarism, and Grant-making Foundations

Do you find often yourself gathering friends and family members to volunteer at a local charity event? Do your children expect every weekend to bring a service project of some sort? Do you feel that it is everyone's social responsibility to help those in need? Do you still hear echoes of President John F. Kennedy's challenge to Americans: "Ask not what your country can do for you, but what you can do for your country"? If you enjoy galvanizing the energy and passion of those around you to change the world, then the philanthropy, voluntarism, and grant-making universe may be for you.

While finding a job in a foundation is difficult, finding a position in a nonprofit that encourages philanthropy or voluntarism is not. Business minds that can leverage relationships and funds, take advantage of technological advances, and package products in new and exciting way will do well here. Some of the most innovative nonprofits today are working to galvanize new energy and resources in the sector.

Philanthropy, Voluntarism, and Grant-making

The philanthropy, voluntarism, and grant-making foundations segment includes:

- **Private grant-making foundations.** Corporate, independent, and operating foundations

- **Public foundations.** Community foundations

- **Voluntarism promotion.** Nonprofits focused on increasing or leveraging volunteering

- **Philanthropy, charity, and voluntarism.** Nonprofits focused on increasing or leveraging philanthropy, charity, and volunteering

- **Federated giving program**

- **Named trusts**

VolunteerMatch. What if, somewhere on the Internet, a community of people gathered who believed in the power of volunteering to enrich our lives and the world around us? What if, somewhere on the Internet, millions of good people and good causes could come together to form relationships that serve us all? What if, somewhere on the Internet, technology was being used to advance the values and partnerships that strengthen our civil society? Well, that somewhere exists at www. volunteermatch.org. Since 1998, VolunteerMatch has been helping volunteers and businesses find local nonprofits by zip code, get involved based on skills and interests, and support a community network committed to civic engagement. Since its founding, VolunteerMatch has helped volunteers make more than 7.4 million matches to more than 96,000 nonprofits throughout the United States.

http://www.volunteermatch.org

Social Venture Partners. Created in Seattle in 1997, Social Venture Partners builds philanthropic communities by using a model that parallels venture capital practices. The first half of the model is investment that builds the long-term capacity of organizations, rather than short-term projects or programs. Investment might include cash grants, skilled volunteers, professional consultants, leadership development, and management training opportunities. Partners make an annual contribution of at least $5,000 and make decisions about how to share their collective investment as well as provide volunteer support in areas such as marketing, finance, technology, strategic planning, and human resources management.

The second half of the model is the mobilization of a community of lifelong, informed, and inspired philanthropists. Through engagement with its nonprofits, connections with other partners, and participation in education events, partners are inspired to reinvest and make new investments in more nonprofit organizations in the future. Currently, Social Venture Partners organizations are in 34 cities around the world, with investments from just under 3,000 individual partners in 2013. *http://www.socialventurepartners.org*

Science and Technology

Do you have fond memories of your early science classes, where your imagination was set afire and the universe was yours to discover? Has your intellectual curiosity been stymied by market whims and financial forces? Have you learned how to utilize technology in ways that have benefited your wallet and the wallets of others, but want to do more? Consider taking your technical expertise to the nonprofit sector, either in an organization focused on science and technology or in the application of science and technology to another social mission.

An easy crossover point for those in the technology arena, this segment is filled with people who crossed over the sector border repeatedly. Those with project management expertise, technical skills, and a deep belief in a social mission will enjoy the work they find here.

Science and Technology

The science and technology segment includes:

- **General science.** Marine science and oceanography are two examples.

- **Physical and earth sciences.** Astronomy, chemistry, mathematics, and geology fall into this category.

- **Engineering and technology.** This includes computer science and engineering.

- **Biological and life sciences**

Following are a couple of nonprofits in the science and technology segment.

Benetech. Founded in 2001, Benetech is a unique bridge that connects the social sector with business and technology leaders. Joining the heart of social mission with the mind of high-tech process and project management, Benetech leverages the vast technical skill base in Silicon Valley to serve humanity. Benetech operates much like a start-up company in a venture capital environment. It identifies needs and opportunities where technology could have a tremendous impact, improving the lives of thousands (potentially millions) of people, and applies research, analysis, and business planning to develop and implement it. Current projects are in the areas of disabilities, human rights, poverty, and education and literacy. *http://benetech.org*

Society for Science & the Public. You may not have heard of this organization, but you certainly remember the science fair. Since 1921, the Society for Science & the Public (SSP) has been encouraging students, parents, teachers, and communities to explore, appreciate, and understand the vast world of science through publications and educational programs. SSP publishes Science News, a weekly magazine, and operates Science for Kids, a popular website for middle school science students. SSP also administers three of the premier science competitions in the county: the Intel Science Talent Search, America's oldest and most highly regarded science contest for high school seniors; the International Science and Engineering Fair, the only worldwide science competition for students in grades 9-12; and the Young Scientists Challenge, which enables middle school children to participate in a national competition that emphasizes the student's ability to communicate about science. Together, these science education programs reach over 3.5 million students worldwide. *https://www.societyforscience.org*

Public/Private Partnerships

Are you a proponent of privatizing public services? Do you think that the world would run more smoothly if only the government and private sector worked together better? Have you spent your career on one side of the private-public fence and have expertise and experience you could lend by hopping to the other side? If so, those organizations serving the public through partnerships or by developing the next generation of public sector leaders may be for you.

Many nonprofits that fuse public-private partnerships rely on the business relationships built by their formerly corporate staff. In addition, they emphasize developing current and new leaders, a mission that nicely complements the background of those in human resources, training, and development.

Let's take a look at three public and societal benefit nonprofits.

The American Legion. The American Legion was chartered by Congress in 1919 as a patriotic veterans' organization. Focusing on service to veterans, servicemembers and communities, the Legion evolved from a group of war-weary veterans of World War I into one of the most influential nonprofit groups in the United States. Membership swiftly grew to over 1 million, and local posts sprang up across the country. Today, membership stands at over 2.4 million in 14,000 posts worldwide, each working to raise money and provide comfort to those

Public/Private Partnerships

Nonprofit that work as public/private partnerships includes:

- Government and public administration

- Military and veterans' organizations

- Public transportation systems

- Telecommunications

- **Financial institutions.** Credit unions are one example.

- Leadership development

- Public utilities

- Consumer protection

who defend our nation.
http://legion.org

American Water Works Association. Founded in 1881, the American Water Works Association (AWWA) is an international nonprofit, scientific, and educational society dedicated to the improvement of water quality and supply. AWWA is the largest organization of water supply professionals in the world, with its more than 57,000 members representing the full spectrum of the water quality community: treatment plant operators and managers, scientists, environmentalists, manufacturers, academicians, regulators, and others. Membership includes more than 4,700 utilities that supply water to roughly 180 million people in North America.
http://www.awwa.org

Consumers Union. Consumers Union is the name you don't know. But you'll recognize its product, Consumer Reports, the magazine you buy

whenever you are about to purchase a large appliance or new vehicle. Since 1936, Consumer Reports has been the most trusted name in unbiased advice about products and services, personal finance, health and nutrition, and other consumer concerns. For nearly 80 years they have tested products, informed the public, and protected consumers with income derived solely from the sale of Consumer Reports and other services, never from advertising or sponsorships.
http://consumersunion.org

Religious Nonprofits

You may already volunteer through your place of worship. But have you ever thought of making a career out of it? Religious nonprofits include the obvious—churches, synagogues, and mosques—but also organizations supporting missionary or evangelical work and publishing, gift shops, or other auxiliary activities.

Religious organizations fund their proselytizing and spiritual work through fundraising efforts; membership fees; and sales of books, gifts, spiritual travel, or other profitable ventures. In other words, despite being thousands of years old, religion today is very much an entrepreneurial effort. Further, with the government placing more of the burden of human services on faith-based communities—as well as opening up new streams of funding for them—religious organizations have become a dominant force within the social sector. Just as there may be a place for religion in your business mind, there can be a place for a business mind in your religion.

Many religion-related nonprofits, such as your neighborhood places of worship, are instantly recognizable and need no further explanation. Instead, let's look at other ways people bring the love of their faith and their corporate expertise to the nonprofit sector.

American Friends Service Committee. The American Friends Service Committee (AFSC) carries out service, development, social justice, and peace programs throughout the world. Founded by Quakers in 1917 to provide conscientious objectors with an opportunity to aid

> **Religion**
>
> **The religion-related segment includes:**
>
> - **Religion-specific nonprofits.** Support of Christianity, Judaism, Islam, Buddhism, Hinduism, and other religions
>
> - **Religious media and communications.** Film and video, television, printing and publishing, Internet, and radio
>
> - **Interfaith coalitions.** These may aim at reconciliation and peace, dialog, or mutual support.

civilian war victims, AFSC's work attracts the support and partnership of people of many races, religions, and cultures. AFSC's work is based on the Quaker belief in the worth of every person and faith in the power of love to overcome violence and injustice. The organization's mission and achievements won worldwide recognition in 1947, when it accepted the Nobel Peace Prize with the British Friends Service Council on behalf of all Quakers. The AFSC is directed by a Quaker board and staffed by Quakers and other people of faith who share the Friends' desire for peace and social justice.
http://afsc.org

The Interfaith Alliance. The Interfaith Alliance (TIA) was founded in 1994 to challenge the radical religious right, and it remains committed to promoting the positive and healing role of religion in public life by encouraging civic participation, facilitating community activism, and challenging religious political extremism. TIA strives to protect both the sanctity of religion and the integrity of government, using religion's power to unite rather than divide. Its members, totaling roughly 185,000, are people of faith, good will, and conscience drawn from more than 75 different religions and belief systems, including individuals who subscribe to no faith tradition. TIA's grassroots base now includes 75 local activist groups in communities across the country and an extensive online action network.
http://www.interfaithalliance.org

Mutual-Membership Benefit

Have you recently retired and begun collecting your pension? Ever wondered how that pension operates or how it was put together? Have you noticed that your regular Thursday nights at "the lodge" seem to be increasingly gray-haired? Want to get some fresh blood into the pipeline but don't have the time with your day job? Perhaps you could turn that hobby into a career in the mutual-membership benefit segment of the nonprofit sector.

Typical transitioners are people with experience running company benefit programs, employee education programs, or local community partnerships. In addition, those with investing and financial sales and advisory expertise can find themselves either on the front lines or in the back office of one of the many benefits firms.

Following are a couple of nonprofits in the mutual-membership benefit segment.

Armed Services Mutual Benefit Association. The Armed Services Mutual Benefit Association (ASMBA) provides comprehensive,

---

Mutual-Membership Benefit

The mutual-membership benefit segment includes:

- **Insurance providers.** Worker's compensation associations, mutual insurance companies, and local benevolent life insurance associations

- **Pension and retirement funds.** Teacher retirement fund associations, employee-funded pension trusts, and multiemployer pension plans

- **Fraternal societies.** Orders, councils, societies, chapters and unions—secret and not—where members come together for a shared purpose

- **Cemeteries and burial services**

---

affordable life insurance coverage to military personnel and their families. ASMBA was established in 1963 by military personnel headed for Vietnam who wanted to provide for their families' security but couldn't get insurance coverage because they were going into a war zone. So they created ASMBA, a nonprofit fraternal military benefit association, which provides security and peace of mind for members of the armed services and their families. And because the value of a life is not determined by rank or branch of service, ASMBA's founders made life insurance plans available to all ranks of all services, during all times of peace or war, with no rank, duty, or geographical restrictions.
http://www.asmba.com

Teachers Insurance and Annuity Association, College Retirement Equities Fund. Better known by its acronym, TIAA-CREF, this nonprofit has been offering a wide range of investment products and services for employees in the academic, cultural, and research fields for more than 85 years. With a portfolio of $380 billion, their charge is clear: to serve those who serve others by providing them with financial expertise to plan for and live comfortably through retirement.
http://www.tiaa-cref.org

Conclusion

Changing your career requires a long, hard look inward. Are you running toward a new job or away from your current job? In reading this chapter, you likely have solidified the passions you already knew lay inside you, and you may have uncovered some you hadn't realized. Perhaps your imagination is afire with all of the wonderful things you might do in the nonprofit world, from practical plans to dramatic dreams. However, while determining which cause you want to assist or which societal problem you want to solve is a big decision, it is only one of three you will have to make.

Now, let's figure out the rest of your nonprofit equation.

Testimonials from Successful Career Changers:

Andrea Kimmel
Associate Director of Marketing,
Harvard Business School, Cambridge, Massachusetts

Andrea grew up in Revere, Massachusetts, a working-class town outside of Boston where few graduate to an Ivy League education or a Fortune 500 professional pedigree. Yet Andrea had dreams and worked hard to fulfill them. An athletic scholarship to Brown University transported her from a conservative, religious community to a bastion of liberalism, where she had to compete with classmates who had prepped at the world's best schools. "When I got there," she says, "I was light years behind. These students already had what I considered to be a college experience at their private boarding schools. In response, I put my head down and copied what they did." For them, and her, that meant going to Wall Street to become an investment banker.

Andrea put in her requisite three years on Wall Street and then followed the pack to business school. "That's where my path began to diverge," she explains. Upon graduation, Andrea looked for a job in a nonprofit but had a hard time convincing anyone to take a chance on her. She ended up back in the corporate sector at Best Buy in Minneapolis. Even though business school got her out of finance, it didn't get her into the nonprofit sector as she had hoped.

As a member of the strategic marketing group, Andrea was able to turn out work she never thought possible. "I loved my job, and I loved the challenge," she says, "but my husband decided he'd missed his calling as a consultant, and his new job brought us back to Boston." When she inquired back at the business school, she learned of a marketing position that felt immediately right. "I now feel a purpose every day when I get out of bed," says Andrea. "I've had my share of frustrations, but I know that I am making a difference."

What have been Andrea's biggest surprises in the nonprofit sector?

"When I got here, nobody in the office had a corporate marketing mentality," she explains. Andrea immediately was forced to put on the brakes and slow down her approach. "I was surprised at how much I had to build up buy-in around decisions that seemed so intuitive from my corporate life." Now, her colleagues come to her and say, "Let's do this. It's an important idea."

Andrea learned that the nonprofit sector is very political. There is more give and take around each idea. "I found that I could contribute what I knew was a cutting-edge corporate marketing idea," she says, "but that it was worthless unless I learned how to operate in the nonprofit environment."

What has been Andrea's most significant reward?

At the end of the day, Andrea feels that she is accepted for who she is. "I was told early on that my colleagues felt threatened by my capabilities and how much I could get done in a month," she says. "So I started coming to meetings looking less prepared and working less hard, or at least trying to give that impression." She quickly realized how ridiculous that was. Instead, Andrea decided to invest in building relationships.

Working in the nonprofit sector, Andrea has found, is about the people. She feels that people care about each other much more than in the corporate world and that she has been much more comfortable being herself because she invested early in building those relationships.

Andrea's Key Lessons Learned:

- ✓ "No one works just 40 hours work week anymore. If you are going to be married to your job, you might as well love what you do."
- ✓ "Be prepared for change to occur more slowly and for more opinions to be weighed. Do not give up on your work goals, but be willing to change your approach to how you make them happen."
- ✓ "Invest in personal relationships early for maximum long-term benefit."

Ned Eames
Founder and President, Tenacity, Inc.
Boston, Massachusetts

Ned was captain of the San Diego State men's tennis team and played professionally on the ATP satellite tour for three years. He worked for five years in sales and marketing, earned his MBA from Boston University, and then became a management consultant to *Fortune 500* companies. Yet after six years of consulting to some of the largest corporations in the country, Ned was left feeling unfulfilled, constrained by the limited nature of the project-based relationships he had with his clients, and uninspired by the internal competition he found rampant among his colleagues. He began to ask himself some tough questions.

"I needed to do something that not only tapped my business skills and interests but also fed my soul," he says, "so I asked myself where I could be of the most service, given who I am today—not who I wanted to be or who I was supposed to be, but who I really am today." The answer that kept coming back to him, even though it was an answer he'd long fought against, was tennis. "I lived in the housing projects for five years as a child," he explains, "and the life lessons that I got from tennis about winning and losing, humility, discipline, motivations, and attitudes helped make me who I am today." Tennis teaching, however, was something that Ned had hoped to avoid when he left the professional circuit.

Ned founded Tenacity, a Boston-based nonprofit, which provides an intensive youth development program with a focus on literacy, character development, and tennis, enabling at-risk youth to achieve on the court, in the classroom, and in life. Tenacity was born out of a convergence of Ned's personal passion about the life-changing effects of tennis on at-risk youth, his desire to be a social entrepreneur, his professional training around large systems change and organizational development, and renewed public attention on after-school programming policies. To date, Tenacity has raised more than $9 million since its inception in 1999 and has served more than 11,000 children.

Why did Ned choose to start his own nonprofit?

"I had always enjoyed my entrepreneurial management classes in my MBA program," he says, "and knew secretly deep down that I always wanted to start something of my own, so I left my fancy consulting job and my suits behind and started working on my business plan." To start his nonprofit, Ned spent almost two years visiting others whom he considered role models, and he surrounded himself with people who had "good character, lots of contacts, and financial resources . . . but mostly good character." He also picked up 20–30 hours a week of private tennis lessons to pay his rent and buy his groceries until he opened Tenacity's doors.

Why has Tenacity been so successful?

Ned didn't surround himself with a board full of nonprofit types, nor did he take classes in nonprofit management. Tenacity was a perfect blend of his avocation with his vocation. "I lived the experience of growing up poor but also working with Fortune 500 CEOs," he says, "so I know what life is like on both sides." What he brought with him was a deep personal passion, personal credibility, and excellent management skills. Along the way, Ned has allowed his staff and their external partners to help him envision and build the program because, as he says, "In the nonprofit sector, like in the corporate sector, people support what they help create."

Ned's Key Lessons Learned:

- ✓ "I refer to nonprofits as businesses. There are a lot of similarities. You've still got to bring the bucks in and that is a very competitive process oftentimes, and you have to provide a great service."
- ✓ "I felt that I knew a lot about how tennis could help a person grow, having had that life experience, and knew that when I started my program, I would have both legs underneath me in full force."
- ✓ "Work is a big part of your life, so you ought to find something that feeds your soul, something that you want to live every day."

CHAPTER 3:
Nonprofit Trends and Job Profiles

As you have just read, today's nonprofit sector is a vast world of great innovation and variety. That means your new career in the nonprofit sector can encompass service to any number of causes you may wish to address. Yet some nonprofits make for easier transitions than others, and each gives you an opportunity to serve that special cause differently. Certain trends in the sector have made room for many new skill sets—such as yours from the private sector—to find a home. The nonprofits that have internalized these trends allow for smoother transitions than those that have not.

To some, picking a favorite cause is like picking a favorite child. It's a nearly impossible task. Many come to the sector just looking to give back in any way they can. Others have a particular cause in mind. Either way, determining your driving social concern is only one of the three decisions you will need to make. To expedite your transition into the nonprofit sector, you will also have to determine which tactical approach you would like to take in solving your pressing social concern and which nonprofit lifecycle stage best fits with your professional personality. Once you've done that, you will need to make your last major decision, which entails looking at your entire body of work, including both your paid and volunteer experiences, to determine where your skills can best be put to use. Each of these three decisions is equally important. While your gut—with the help of Chapter 2, has likely answered the first already, reading this chapter will help you answer the second and third.

Let's start with some of the trends in the nonprofit world.

Trends in the Nonprofit Sector Are Creating Opportunities for Career Changers

The nonprofit sector is changing every day. As it changes, trends have begun to emerge. These trends point to increased opportunities for those with business skills.

Nonprofit Mergers

In the period between 1996-2006, the number of nonprofits in the United States increased by 64 percent.[16] From 2002-2007, nonprofits saw a 33.5 percent increase in revenues and a 35.2 percent increase in assets, but this growth slowed (only 6.6 percent for revenues, and 5.8 percent for assets) from 2007-2012. Some subsectors did better than others; arts, culture, and humanities organizations, as well an international organizations, have still not recovered from the economic ramifications of the recession.[17] This has forced nonprofits to think about closures, mergers, and acquisitions as a means of continuing to serve the ongoing need of their communities.

The influx of business thinking within nonprofits and a new wave of corporate-minded donors has, in part, fueled nonprofit mergers as a solution to the problem of constricted operating capital. Merged nonprofits find that they can consolidate staff, reduce competition, and minimize overhead costs. This trend is good news for corporate career changers, as merger and acquisition work is uncharted territory for many nonprofit staff.

---

16. \FN\ Sasha Talcott, "Nonprofit Mergers Catch on in Region," Boston Globe, April 6, 2006, *www.boston.com/business/articles/2006/04/06/nonprofit_mergers_catch_in_region/* (accessed November 26, 2006).

17. Urban Institute Center on Nonprofits and Philanthropy, "The Nonprofit Sector in Brief 2014".

Revenue-Generating Subsidiaries

As the competition for funding dollars increases, nonprofits are realizing that they will be more successful if they rely less on the whims of individual donors or government funding and more on themselves. Doing so means that they must come up with new ways to fund their programs. Youth service nonprofits might run fee-for-service summer programs to provide school-year scholarships, transitional houses and long-term shelters might teach their residents the job skills necessary to run a café that funds more beds, and fair trade advocacy groups might sell chocolate made from cocoa harvested by fairly paid workers rather than trafficked children.

Public-Private Partnerships

Nonprofits have learned that it is not enough to work on their own, even if they do outstanding work. Some of the most exciting work in the nonprofit sector today is done in collaboration between the corporate and nonprofit sectors. It seems so simple, but bureaucracy, misunderstandings, and stereotypes have long kept these sectors apart. More and more, nonprofits and corporations are joining together, breaking down barriers of language and culture and creating new and innovative programs.

Focus on Scalability

The new trends in philanthropy—led by dot-com millionaires and venture philanthropists—mean that foundations look at their role in the nonprofit sector entirely differently than they may have twenty years ago. Many foundations still stick to the old way of heavy-handed, slow thinking, but more and more often, foundations are catching on that they can create the change they want to see in the world. In addition, through President Barack Obama's 2009 American Recover and Reinvestment Act (the "stimulus package"), a Social Innovation Fund was created to identify and fund just this sort of work. Empowering nonprofit partners with proven business models to do their work even better, more broadly, and with increased efficiency is an attractive proposition for private funders, foundations, and the government alike. The idea of the nonprofit as a partner, not just the recipient of a carefully constructed, tightly managed grant, is new, and this method of venture thinking (i.e., scalable, demonstrable, innovative, and creative) is most successful with agile and responsive nonprofits. Nonprofits who employ business minds, MBAs, and corporate types have an advantage because they speak the language of the corporate sector, understand the business model, and have worked with others who share the same mentality and benchmarking for success.

Management Matters

With the increasing focus on the bottom line, and with more and more competition for funding, nonprofits are getting wise that management techniques matter. Once considered taboo, nonprofits no longer feel shy about incorporating best practices from the private sector. It is not uncommon to hear a nonprofit executive director discussing some of the latest ideas from famed management gurus, from Jim Collins's ideas (*Good to Great*, and his popular monograph *Good to Great and the Social Sectors*) about getting the right people on the right seat on the bus, for example, or Peter Senge's thoughts (*The Fifth Discipline*) on building learning organizations. Where once such comments would have been met with horror and shock, they now are met with heads nodding in agreement. However, great management in the nonprofit sector means nothing if it is not done compassionately. Corporate managers who can bring the mind of a businessperson coupled with the heart of a social worker will do very well in, and by, the nonprofits they serve.

Now let's find the right nonprofit for you.

Define Your Tactical Approach

As we've discussed, nonprofit organizations are often broken down into the following groups: arts, culture, and humanities; education; environment and animals; health; human services; international and foreign affairs; public and societal benefit; religion-related; mutual and membership benefit. In each of these groups, the water is a little muddy;

for example, a historical museum may hold the world's largest collection of 16th-century Scottish armor but have as one of its central purposes the education of young children. Organizations are defined by how they describe themselves in their applications for tax-exempt status, not their brand identity.

Legally Defined Categories of Nonprofits

Most of the 1.5 million registered nonprofits in the United States fall into one of a few categories. They are public charities, advocacy-lobbying organizations, or membership associations.

Public Charities—501(c)(3)s

The just under 1 million public charities in the United States fall into a few distinct groups:

- **Social service organizations**. The driving principle of these public charities is simply the betterment of others through delivery of some sort of service or good. These organizations include Easter Seals, the American Red Cross, and your local food bank, library, or homeless shelter.

- **Foundations**. Foundations exist to fund specific types of activities of nonprofits or individuals, as defined by their mission statements or charters. Social service organizations work to create hands-on change in these areas, while foundations fund their work. Foundations range from the largest, like the Ford Foundation or the Gates Foundation, to the small community foundations in cities and towns nationwide.

- **Support/capacity-building organizations**. As the nonprofit sector becomes more organized, a new level of nonprofits has arisen to support their work. Like the corporate sector, which has legions of consultants and outside experts, the nonprofit sector now, too, benefits from management support organizations and board training centers to accomplish their goals. You may know these organizations as the United Way, CompassPoint, or Board Source.

Social Welfare Organizations and Local Employee Associations—
501(c)(4)s

Civic Leagues and local employee associations operated for the promotion of social welfare fall into this broad category. Mostly political in nature, these organizations exist to sway public or elected opinion to change existing public policy or upcoming legislation. Different from political action committees (PACs), 501(c)(4)s do not work specifically on behalf of or against a particular candidate for public office but may take a stand on them depending on whether or not they agree on the issues. Also, unlike political action committees, these 501(c)(4) organizations must file returns with the IRS. Nearly 86,500 of these organizations are registered with the Internal Revenue Service (IRS), including Greenpeace, the National Rifle Association, the American Federation of Teachers, and NARAL.

Membership Associations—501(c)(6)s

These professional organizations represent members brought together because of a shared trade, skill, area of focus, or career path. These include individual membership and trade organizations like the National Association of Realtors or entities like the National Council of Nonprofit Associations, itself an association of local and state nonprofit associations.

Additional Classifications for Nonprofits

In addition to these three categories, into which most nonprofits fall, there are more than 30 additional IRS classifications for credit unions, pensions, workers compensation reinsurance, black lung benefit trusts, and the like. These can be found at *www.irs.gov/Charities-&-Non-Profits/* *Types-of-Tax-Exempt-Organizations.*

Minor but Major Differences

Advocacy organizations and trade associations will, of course, tell you that they are serving a social purpose, and they are. However, the line between them exists because of IRS rules about how donated money can be spent.

Money given to a 501(c)(3), such as the American Red Cross or the Girl Scouts, can be used to deliver goods and services to, but not advocate on behalf of, individuals or causes. Money given to a 501(c)(4), such as Handgun Control or the National Rifle Association, can be used for advocacy. Donations made to a 501(c)(3) are tax-deductible, while donations made to a 501(c)(4) are not. Some 501(c)(3)s define their outreach work as "educational," but if the work gets close to a dangerous line (losing nonprofit status for violations is no laughing matter), some 501(c)(3) and 501(c)(6) nonprofits set up separate 501(c)(4) organizations to fundraise and spend entirely separately from their service delivery arms.

The AARP is a well-known nonprofit that registers part of its organization as a 501(c)(3), part as a 501(c)(4), and yet another part as a 501(c)(6). Individuals can join AARP when they reach the ripe old age of 50 and begin receiving travel discounts, tax preparation help, driver safety courses, a monthly magazine, and all sorts of other benefits. They are given opportunities to donate their time in the many social service-driven AARP volunteer programs. The AARP touts the voting power of its more than 37 million members in the halls of Congress. And so, the AARP, and its foundation and membership subsidiaries, exists as a public charity, a membership association, and an advocacy organization.

Another interesting example is Google.org, the foundation started by founders of the popular search engine Google. With $1 billion in funding and a program direction aimed at global poverty reduction, energy, and the environment, it sounds like any other large foundation—except for one thing: Google.org has organized itself as a corporate entity, meaning that it pays taxes but it can also raise and disburse money to nonprofits or corporations and use its considerable muscle to lobby on behalf of the causes it funds.

Different Nonprofit Tactics

Each nonprofit takes a different approach to solving a societal problem. Determining your place in the sector demands that you think about which approach leverages your interest and transferrable skills.

For example: Nearly one in three adult women experience at least one physical assault by a partner during adulthood. It's a problem of outrageous proportions, and no single approach can solve it. Below, the tactics of different types of nonprofits can illustrate the importance of approach.

Direct service →

- Twenty-four hour hotlines, counseling services, and transitional housing, allowing victims to escape quickly and anonymously
- Interview training and professional clothing swaps for newly single mothers seeking first-time employment

Philanthropy →

- Immediate cash gifts for first month's rent and security deposits on new apartments, enabling women to move themselves and their children away from an abusive partner
- For organizations, grants made to fund new programs, more first-line responders, or public affairs campaigns

Support and capacity building →

- Training of volunteers to become counselors to victims, in long-term relationships that provide stability and support
- Donations of and training on new computer systems or telephone systems that enable first-line responders to access historical data quickly on each relationship

Lobbying and advocacy →

- Public education campaigns about the affects of alcohol and drug abuse, economic downturns, or other factors linked to spikes in the incidence of domestic violence, or about the increase in domestic attacks on men
- Recent legislative action that makes marital rape a crime

Membership organizations →

- Pooled benefits for women previously trapped in abusive relationships because of the need for health insurance for sick children
- Support groups for victims and children

Note about Foundation Jobs

Many career changers come to the nonprofit sector in search of a job in a foundation. Such positions seem, from the outside, to be the ultimate dream jobs. Foundations gave an estimated $45.74 billion in 2012 alone.[18] Who doesn't want to spend their days giving away someone else's money?

However, foundation jobs are notoriously difficult to get. Foundations have very little turnover. There are fewer foundations than other nonprofits—5.1 percent of the entire sector[19]—so there are fewer foundation jobs than there are other nonprofit jobs. In fact, foundations employ less than 0.5 percent of the workers in the nonprofit sector.[20] Corporate foundations tend to hire from within their own ranks, typically from retiring executives or marketing and public relations senior staff. Private foundations are often looking for people with deep field experience or a Ph.D, or sometimes both, in the field or fields that they fund. It is certainly worth pursuing a position at a foundation if that's what you truly desire, but keep in mind that your job search may take longer than you expect.

The grant-making world may also not be a good fit for the transitioner job seeker's point of view. Many foundations are slow and deliberative, often thinking and writing about subjects for years before determining funding priorities. Many are filled with academic types who are not sensitive to, or simply not interested in, the whims of the market. Staffs tend to be small, and individuals spend gobs of time alone in their offices reading proposals or other research-driven publications.

Corporate transitioners who insist on finding the holy grail of a foundation job would be well advised to look towards newer foundations, those founded by dot-com millionaires and venture capitalists like Bill Gates, Pierre Omidyar, and Jeff Skoll, which do not share the

---

18. Giving USA, *Charitable Donations Grew in 2012, but Slowly, Like the Economy*, (http://www.philanthropy. iupui.edu/news/article/giving-usa-2013.

19. \FN\ Independent Sector, *National Almanac of Nonprofit Statistics in Brief*, (Washington, D.C.: Independent Sector, 1998): 5.

20. \FN\ Independent Sector, *Nonprofit Almanac*, (Washington, D.C.: Independent Sector, 2001): 9.

typical traits of older, more staid foundations. This new wave of young philanthropists is applying lessons from the private sector to address social needs. They see themselves not as ATMs for nonprofits but as partners, being hands-on when they make grants, and as risk takers, venturing money on unproven but exciting ideas rather than the same old service delivery model.

Job Titles in the Nonprofit Sector

Job titles in the nonprofit sector can be confusing. They don't correlate with those in the corporate sector; for example, you are unlikely to find a total quality improvement specialist, a business analyst, or a loan support processing supervisor in most organizations. Similarly, you won't find an organic farmer, a community organizer, or a home detention caseworker in the corporate sector. And just what is a program officer, anyway? Figures A and B show two possible organizational charts, one for a larger nonprofit and one for a smaller nonprofit.

Job postings may have seemingly senior titles that don't, in reality, give the employee much authority. Many directors in the nonprofit sector are directors of their own work and precious little else. Make sure you research each job listing thoroughly to ensure that your experience is aligned with the substance of a job, instead of applying for positions based on titles alone.

Generally, nonprofit titles can be grouped into several functional areas of work: management; programs; fundraising; communications; and administration, operations, and finance. Let's look at each of these areas in more detail.

The Management Team

Executive Director, President, or Chief Executive Officer

The executive director is often the chief professional officer of a nonprofit. Sometimes the executive director (ED) is called the president or the chief executive officer (CEO). A nonprofit that is more in touch with its business side is one that has a CEO rather than an ED.

The chief professional officer, whom we will call the executive director for the balance of this section, is hired by and reports to the board of directors (always a volunteer group in the nonprofit sector). The ED's job is broken down into four main areas of responsibility:

1. **Management.** The buck stops at the executive director. The ED has overall responsibility for hiring and firing, setting the organization's strategic direction, implementing its business plan, capitalizing on new opportunities, and overseeing the budget.

2. **Program oversight.** Nonprofits exist to serve a cause; that cause is reflected in the programs they provide. The executive director has a hand in creating, designing, implementing, prioritizing, and evaluating programs. The ED also decides when new programs will be launched and when the lifespan of an old program is over.

3. **Communications.** Depending on the nonprofit and its mission, communications might be called public relations, public affairs, lobbying, public education, or external relations. Regardless of its nomenclature, this function includes the responsibility of being chief spokesperson of the organization.

4. **Fundraising.** Last, but certainly not least, the chief professional officer of any nonprofit spends a good deal of time every day raising money.

Deputy Director, Associate Director, Vice President, or Chief Operating Officer

Small nonprofits—those under $250,000 in budget—often rely solely on an executive director. Larger nonprofits—from $1,000,000 and above—have a more fleshed-out senior management team. Somewhere in the middle, nonprofits realize that they are big enough to warrant a deputy director or vice president. This usually happens as the executive directors of start-ups or growing nonprofits find that they are spending

Figure A.
Sample Organization Chart for a Larger Nonprofit:

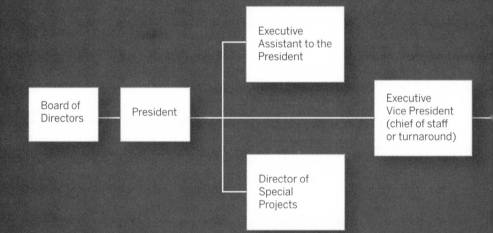

```
Vice President
of Programs
    ├── Director of
    │   Programs ──────────── Subordinates:
    │                         individual site,
    │                         location, or
    │                         program managers
    │
    └── Director of
        Assessment and ────── Subordinates:
        Evaluation            training and
                              technical assist.,
                              grants manager

Vice President
of Administration
and Finance
    ├── Director of
    │   Finance ──────────── Subordinates:
    │                         accountant,
    │                         comptroller,
    │                         bookkeeper
    │
    └── Director of
        Operations ────────── Subordinates:
                              office manager,
                              HR, technology,
                              receptionist

Vice President
of Development
    ├── Director of
    │   Development ───────── Subordinates:
    │                         major gifts, events,
    │                         alumni relations,
    │                         grant writing
    │
    └── Director of
        Business ──────────── Subordinates:
        Development           revenue generation,
                              earned income,
                              subsidiaries

Vice President of
Communications
    ├── Director of
    │   Strategic ─────────── Subordinates:
    │   Communications        public affairs,
    │                         marketing,
    │                         branding, writing
    │
    └── Director of
        Public Affairs ────── Subordinates:
                              advocacy, lobbying,
                              strategic partnerships,
                              research, events
```

Figure B.
Sample Organization Chart for a Small Nonprofit:

Board of Directors

Executive Director

Executive Assistant to the President:
Some executive directors of smaller nonprofits forgo the salary of an executive assistant and instead put the money toward a part-time grant writer or other staff member

Director of Programs:
Work includes all program design, implementation, and evaluation and provision of training and technical assistance to staff, volunteers, or sites, and often includes active participation in all grant writing activities

Director of Operations:
Work includes all finance, administration, and operations related to making the office run smoothly and remain in compliance

Director of Development and Communications:
Work includes all external relations such as fundraising and strategic partnership creation, major gifts, events, alumni relations, grants

more time on developing the organization's vision and raising money and less time on the structures and procedures that nonprofits need to withstand change and flourish.

Deputy directors may take on the chief operations officer role or may be the chief program director, or they may be both. Each nonprofit defines these roles differently. Generally speaking, all oversight for executive, programming, fundraising, and operational functions usually reside with the executive director and the deputy director.

Some nonprofits take this a step further, anointing the board chair as president, or moving a founder into a president's role, while making the executive director the chief professional officer. In these cases, the structure follows the same internal-external division of duties between a president and a vice president that you find in the corporate sector.

The Senior Management Team

Rounding out the senior management team are, along with the executive director and the deputy director, the chiefs of all major areas of the organization. This normally includes—in nonprofits large enough to have all of these positions—the director of programs, the director of fundraising, the director of operations, the director of administration and finance, and the director of communications. Because nonprofits tend to collapse more functions into fewer positions, you may find that all of these positions are represented with fewer bodies. These functions are described in the sections that follow.

The Program Team

Corporations make money through the sale of products or services. Nonprofits spend money in the output of products or services. Those products or services are distributed through the programs of the nonprofit. This doesn't mean that the position of product manager or service manager in the corporate sector corresponds directly to that of program officer or program manager of a nonprofit. It may sit in the same place on the organizational chart and carry out similar functions, but the knowledge required for the position is quite different. Most program staff hold a deep understanding of the subject matter of the nonprofit's programs, have worked in the community for years, and are deeply ingrained in the relevant issues. Because of this required knowledge base, program positions are some of the hardest for career changers to transition into, and even when secured, they often result in the least successful transitions.

The program team may be one person or one person per site, or it may consist of several individuals. The program staff of a nonprofit is responsible for the following:

- **Program design.** The architecture of a program is a major factor in its ultimate success or failure. Nonprofits are given awards and positive public attention for innovation in program design, leading to increased financial support.

- **Program implementation.** Efficiency in program implementation matters, despite what you may hear. The better the implementation, the better the results.

- **Program assessment and evaluation.** Like private sector investors, funders demand bang for their buck. Rather than seeing return on investment (ROI) in terms of dollars, funders see the return as numbers of immunizations delivered or houses built.

The Fundraising Team

The smaller the nonprofit, the more likely that the executive director is the entire fundraising team (also known as the development team) for the organization. Given that the executive director is the chief spokesperson and champion for the cause, it makes sense that this position will play a key role in all major funder relationships. As nonprofits grow, most will bring on a fundraising associate, prospect research assistant, or grant writer before bringing on a development director.

The senior staff in a nonprofit wakes up in the morning and goes to bed at night thinking about how to raise more money. The fundraising team is responsible for bringing in the dollars by one method or another. They may be accountable for the following:

- **Event management.** Large nonprofits, and especially old nonprofits, tend to host a plethora of events designed as both fundraisers and "friendraisers." With the exception of the major galas you might read about in The New York Times Styles section, fundraising events tend not to bring in large amounts of money, but they do reinvigorate constituents and introduce new people to the organization.

- **Grant writing.** Most foundations award funds through a long, drawn-out grant application process. They put out requests for proposals (RFPs) and often ask applicants to jump through multiple hoops to apply. Grant writing is both a skill and an art, and career changers who learn about it will be well served.

- **Major gifts.** Major gifts are just what they sound like: major gifts from private individuals or corporations. This type of fundraising might come most naturally to a career changer, in that it is similar to one-on-one sales pitches they may have experience with.

- **Direct mail.** Nonprofits also raise money through direct mail solicitations. These tend to be annual drives, often conducted in December to take advantage of donors looking for tax breaks.

- **Capital campaigns.** Capital campaigns are one-time, large fund drives focused on the purchase or improvement of a physical space, like a building or a playground.

- **Membership development.** Finally, people are needed to recruit and retain members. Because donations to a membership organization are not tax deductible, but the cost of membership might be, the membership development professional is tasked with bringing in the money to fund programs.

Fundraisers tend to move around a lot, and nonprofits are always looking for good ones. If you look on any nonprofit job board, you will find an overwhelming number of development jobs. Other than the executive director, the director of development is often the highest-paid individual on staff; in some cases they make even more than the executive director. Some nonprofits, to justify the high salaries demanded by fundraising professionals, combine fundraising and communications under one external affairs umbrella.

The Communications Team

Depending on the nonprofit and its mission, communications might be called public relations, public affairs, lobbying, public education, marketing, or external relations. Regardless of its nomenclature, communications includes the following functions:

- **Media relations.** In public advocacy nonprofits, great emphasis is put on issuing press releases and placing stories in print, television, radio, and Internet outlets.

- **Public education or lobbying.** If crossed, this tricky line could comprise a nonprofit's tax status. Therefore, nonprofits are careful to ensure that they are either informing the public about issues and leaving the action to them or directly lobbying for policy change at local, state, or national levels.

- **Public affairs.** Nonprofits use all sorts of methods to get the word out. This can span the spectrum from direct marketing to public education.

- **Membership services.** In associations, the membership services coordinator is the first line of interaction between members and the organization. Like the executive director, the membership staff act as public faces for the nonprofit.

- **Online functions.** These constitute a whole new set of roles for nonprofits, despite their existence in the corporate sector for years. These jobs most likely are bundled together to include website design, programming, blogs, donation databases, and more.

In most nonprofit organizations, the executive director and the director of development are both very public faces. Because of that, the emphasis on communications functions has lagged behind that in the corporate sector, though a number of nonprofits now seek a new model of communicator known as the "Movement Builder," who can popularize an issue and build a groundswell of grassroots support to change social norms and incite action on behalf of a cause. Even in nonprofits without a director of communications, there may be several of these other sub-functions. Where there is no director of communications, they may report to the director of development or a director of external relations.

The Administrative, Financial, and Operations Team

Given that nonprofits tend to lag far behind their corporate counterparts in structures and systems, it probably won't surprise you

---

The Hierarchy of Nonprofit Jobs

Titles in the nonprofit sector differ from titles in the corporate sector. Below, from most senior to least senior, is a sample hierarchy of titles:

- **Executive director, president, chief executive officer** (often interchangeable)
- **Deputy director, associate director, vice president, chief professional officer** (often interchangeable)
- **Senior director or senior officer**
- **Director or officer**
- **Manager**
- **Coordinator**
- **Associate**
- **Assistant**

Remember, in the nonprofit sector, raises and bonuses are harder to come by. As a result, nonprofits freely inflate titles. Beware the nonprofit where a director only needs three to five years of experience—unless, of course, you have four.

---

to know that many nonprofits lump administrative, financial, and operations functions together in one or just a few individuals. This is where the attraction of the nonprofit sector to generalists is the strongest. While no one expects that the accountant will know how to disperse employee benefits, nonprofits simply may have one person overseeing the functions of several part-time staffers or consultants who fill these needs.

That all being said, larger nonprofits have begun investing more and more in their infrastructure and the result has been a more professionalized view of the administrative, financial, and operations functions of their organizations. Career changers will find that, despite a few new compliance rules to learn, their most natural transition happens in the following functions:

- **Accounting and financial.** The CPA or bookkeeper on board—and yes, these jobs do sometimes fall into a bookkeeper's hands in a smaller nonprofit—might handle all grant disbursement, accounts payable and accounts receivable tasks, overall responsibility for profit and loss, and the annual audit.

- **Operations.** Those who oversee operations can be anything from office managers—ensuring that supplies are always in stock—to facilitators of strategic planning. When nonprofits look to relocate offices, implement organizational policies and procedures, and streamline functions, they turn to the operations people.

- **Legal/general counsel.** Few nonprofits are large enough to have an in-house lawyer. Those who do house them in the office of the general counsel.

- **Human resources/staffing.** Depending on the size of the nonprofit or the amount of hiring it does each year, nonprofits will outsource or bring in-house a human resources and/or recruiting function. Larger nonprofits with national offices and local affiliates tend to house human resources in central locations. More forward-thinking nonprofits place professional training and development in these functions as well. However, you'll be surprised at how many job postings list the executive director as the recipient of all résumés.

- **Executive assistance.** Anyone in the secretarial pool or working as an executive assistant may report directly to his or her manager, or they may be part of an overall customer service team. Because of the nature of nonprofits, even some of the most senior players may find themselves changing the toner on the copier from time to time.

- **Information technology.** Like online functions, nonprofits more and more are bringing IT experts in-house, an acknowledgment that their work is becoming increasingly data and technology driven. The crossover of skills in this area is clear, although corporate transitioners may be shocked at the rudimentary technology they discover on their nonprofit desk.

Consulting Services

Tens of thousands of people make their living consulting to the nonprofit sector, as a nonprofit or corporate employee themselves, either individually or within a larger firm, in one or more of the capacities outlined above. In fact, many career changers find themselves consulting either as a volunteer or in a paid capacity during their job search; some find themselves so successful that they forget about the job search altogether and remain a consultant as long as the pipeline of work remains full.

As with anything, there are positives and negatives to being an independent consultant in the nonprofit sector. On the downside, consulting can be an isolating experience and, at times, a frustrating one. Consultants often complain that they not only miss the water cooler banter of the office environment but that they hardly ever get to see their work product implemented and, therefore, don't get to share in the celebration or reflection. On the other hand, individual consultants may set their own hours, choose their own clients, and offer only the services they enjoy providing.

Examples of Corporate and Nonprofit Consulting Firms

Corporate transitioners looking to move into more traditional consulting within the nonprofit space should look at the various corporate and nonprofit consulting firms springing up around the country. Here are some examples on the corporate side, although certainly many assignments are done at cost, heavily discounted, or even pro bono:

- **McKinsey and Company's Nonprofit Practice.** Using consultants from across their industry practices, McKinsey's nonprofit clients experience the prototypical McKinsey approach, but at reduced fees. McKinsey chooses its clients based on potential impact. It makes fee decisions based on ability to pay, yet it feels that paying something increases client commitment to the effort.

- **Isaacson, Miller.** A national executive search firm, Isaacson, Miller undertakes searches for a wide variety of organizations, including leading universities, research institutes, academic medical centers, foundations, cultural institutions, economic development organizations, human service agencies, national advocacy groups, and socially responsible businesses.

- **Accounting Management Solutions.** Based in New England, this outsourcing, recruiting, and interim financial management company brings businesslike practices to the nonprofit sector with industry-trained, experienced, short- or long-term accounting personnel who implement current best practices.

- **New Profit, Inc.** New Profit provides performance-based funding coupled with strategic resources to maximize the social impact and sustainability of other nonprofit organizations.

- **Nonprofit Professionals Advisory Group.** This is the search firm I founded in 2002. We work with nonprofits around the world to ensure that they are thinking strategically about their talent pipeline.

Typical Services Offered by Nonprofit Consultants

Administrative, financial, and operations:

- Accounting, bookkeeping, or other back-office services

- Insurance and risk management

- Online functions

- Software and Web development

- Information systems management

- Fund management

- Endowment management

- Financial management

- Operations management

Executive-level support:

- Coaching and mentoring

- Peer learning

- Executive transition

- Change management

- Temporary staffing (e.g., interim directors)

Fundraising:

- Annual campaigns

- Event planning

- Grant writing

- Fund development

- Strategic development planning

Communications:

- Communications, branding, or graphic design

- Publications

- Writing and editing

- Public relations and marketing

Board development and support:

- Retreat planning and facilitation

- Board and volunteer placement

- Board development

Organizational development:

- Cross-cultural awareness and diversity training

- Capacity building

- Executive search

- Training, workshops, and seminars

- Group facilitation

- Mediation

- Organizational development and assessment

Program support:

- Survey research

- Research

- Evaluation and assessment

Becoming a Consultant to the Nonprofit Sector

Consulting positions within the nonprofit sector, either through a corporate or nonprofit business model, are attractive to former consultants, project managers, or strategists in the corporate sector. Experience with a nonprofit as a board member or through a previous client relationship is a must, because coming to the sector cold with only business expertise provides a limited perspective. That said, many corporate consultants have had at least some exposure to the nonprofit sector through their firm's pro bono work.

Many training programs are available for those interested in impacting the nonprofit sector through a consulting approach. The Institute for Nonprofit Consulting, run by CompassPoint for the past eight years, is a three-day training program. It is designed specifically to help nonprofit consultants establish a framework and strengthen their skills in an approach called client-centered consulting. Third Sector New England presents its annual Nonprofit Workout conference, complete with training sessions for nonprofit consultants. In addition, most state nonprofit associations provide training calendars for both nonprofit managers and consultants alike; attending these trainings enables you to register in their database as a consultant available for hire.

Opening Your Consulting Practice Doors

Once you've established yourself as a consultant to the nonprofit sector, you can register your practice at these sites, to name but a few:

- **Idealist.org** (www.idealist.org)

- **Management Consulting Services** (www.managementconsultingservices.org)

- **Executive Service Corps Affiliate Network** (www.escus.org)

- **CharityChannel** (www.charitychannel.com)

Which Nonprofit Is Right for You?

Now that you have given some thought to what type of approach you would like your nonprofit work to take—direct service, advocacy, or support—and the type of cause to which you would like to dedicate your work, let's add one more layer to the decision-making process. In addition to choosing the direction of the work and the mission that interests you, consider the environment in which you want to work. For most career changers, the environment and kind of work are as important, if not more so, in guiding eventual success or failure than passion for the nonprofit's particular mission.

Like the corporate world, the nonprofit sector is made up of many different types of nonprofits. Like your corporate job, the personality of your employer or workplace supported your successes or created challenges. The nonprofit sector will be the same. Your job search will be shorter, and your tenure on the job will be more enjoyable, if you determine early on which type of nonprofit is the right match for you.

Nonprofits have personalities all their own. Choosing the right kind of nonprofit matters. Depending on your corporate experience, you may be more comfortable in a large organization with built-in practices and administrative support rather than a small, grassroots nonprofit where each employee is chief, cook, and bottle washer. Or, if your experience has been in smaller environments where each person manages his or her own portfolio and reaps the rewards of his or her own success, you may enjoy the scrappiness of a bootstrapping, community-based, grassroots nonprofit, where existence is hand-to-mouth but big changes seem up-close and personal. Nonprofit start-ups are a whole other animal, resembling the gambles of the for-profit sector start-up but with an entirely different payoff.

Your Nonprofit Personality Match

If you need an environment that gives support and stability, you may wish to choose a nonprofit that has been around for many years. If you thrive on chaos and change, you might like an organization that is just getting started, where funding is uncertain and impact is untested, or one that follows a political calendar, with a rebirth each new campaign season. You may be more contemplative and thoughtful, so an academic or foundation environment might suit you best. But if pondering ideas endlessly might make you crazy, a more nimble, fast-acting organization might be the one for you.

Finally, if you are making this transition to be closer to the action, and that action might be described as the hands-on helping of people, then you should choose a grassroots-based nonprofit. If you want to get into the big meetings with decision makers, you might be better served by looking for a job in a smaller, flatter organization.

Refer to Figure C to get a better grasp on the type of nonprofit for which you are suited. Check marks signify that you are likely to find a given characteristic in the type of organization listed above.

The Nonprofit Organization's Life Cycle

As in business, nonprofit organizations have a life cycle. They can either just be starting out (which may or may not be founder driven), transitioning to their mezzanine level, experiencing radical growth, have set a steady and stable course, or be in their decline. Each of these phases brings a different challenge.

Nonprofits enter and exit each of these phases more often because of crises than due to planning. Most nonprofits are so focused on fulfilling their mission and helping their constituents that they pay precious little attention to their own governance and structure. Making matters more complicated is the abundance of managers and leaders in the sector who either don't value or don't understand the importance of internal systems building. Then there's the pesky problem of getting funders to pay for things like long-range strategic planning, even when the nonprofits know it makes sense. All of that being said, many nonprofits get it, do it, and thrive because of it. As you might imagine, these nonprofits will likely be more inviting to those with business résumés.

	Grassroots	Strong and stable	Growth-oriented	In Transition	Start-up	Founder-driven
Decision-making Style:						
I enjoy contemplative environments where ideas are vetted thoroughly before decisions are made.	✓	✓	✓	✓		
I prefer decisions to be made quickly, sometimes with gut-level reactions.		✓	✓	✓		
I like to make decisions on my own.			✓	✓	✓	✓
I seek input from large groups of people before making a final choice.	✓	✓	✓			✓
I do not enjoy making decisions and am happiest following others' leads.		✓				✓
Pace of Workplace:						
I enjoy an office environment where people stop to chat.	✓	✓		✓		✓
I would rather get my work done quickly than standaround and waste time.			✓	✓	✓	✓
Support Network:						
I enjoy multitasking, taking on multiple projects, and working autonomously.	✓			✓	✓	
I need the support of others around me to operate at the highest level.		✓	✓			✓
Structure:						
I work best in a structured environment where decision-making methods are clear.		✓	✓	✓		
I enjoy a more free-form atmosphere where decisions are made by whomever is in the room at the time.	✓			✓	✓	✓

Start-Up

Most nonprofit start-ups are just that: nonprofits that are just starting up. But don't be fooled into thinking that only young nonprofits are in start-up mode. Nonprofits are forced to reinvent themselves every so often, either in response to world affairs, donor whims, market forces, or major personnel changes. At these times and, of course, when they are just starting out, they may find themselves taking on the characteristics of a nonprofit in start-up mode.

Start-up nonprofits look similar to start-up corporations. Money is uncertain, the vision is ambitious, and failure is not an option. Donors must be placated about the probability of success, often without a track record as evidence of potential accomplishment. The board may or may not be a rubber-stamping board, gathered together quickly to submit IRS paperwork. Staff has to work in an "all hands on deck" capacity, often leading to a mismatch of resources and energies.

Still, start-ups happen every day and often produce some of the most exciting and innovative work going on in the nonprofit sector. The Charles Schwab Foundation provides social entrepreneur awards, as does *Fast Company* magazine, in partnership with the Monitor Group, to some of these innovators. Those with corporate backgrounds are well suited to these start-ups, because the pace is normally quicker than entrenched organizations and the opportunity to create systems and structure from the ground up exists in spades.

In Transition

At a certain point in every nonprofit start-up, the staff, board, and other stakeholders realize that explosive start-up growth can only be managed for so long. Pairing continued growth with the continued execution of high-quality service is difficult at best. Nonprofits in transition are no longer adding new locations, for example, and are instead starting to serve more people in a specified area or provide better quality or additional services to existing numbers.

105

Nonprofits in transition often find themselves with a leadership change, whether voluntary or forced. The dynamism and charisma of a founder or of a founding executive director is not necessarily part of the skill set needed to establish the organization in known territory. Few founders relish spending their time examining systems and structures to make sure that their organization can withstand any looming difficulties. Most would rather spend their time acting as an ambassador for their great idea, an advocate on behalf of the cause they serve, or as a champion raising money of its behalf. In truth, such activities are the highest and best use of their time, so having them stick around as an executive director while their organization is in transition is detrimental to everything they have built.

Nonprofits in transition tend to be three to seven years past their start-up mode. They are often on their second or even third executive director, and they have begun adding senior staff positions, like operations, finance, or administration directors. They may likely also be adding development as a full-time role for the first time, because the outgoing founder did all that personally. Great opportunities exist for corporate career changers in these organizations, as long as you don't try to transition the organization too quickly.

Growth-Oriented

Growth-oriented nonprofits are either looking to add more cities, deepen their impact, or improve their quality. They are being pushed by their funders or by their business plan, if they have one, to grow larger. They have likely gotten a larger grant to do more or similar work in a new location or have identified a hole in the services provided to their targeted population and are seeking to fill it.

Often, nonprofits moving from start-up through transition into growth mode do not have the systems and structure in place to support them at this larger level. In some cases, the existing systems and structures simply can't handle larger demands. Change can and should be made in these nonprofits, but even in growth mode, culture shift takes time.

Growth-oriented nonprofits must be careful about "mission drift," which ails nonprofits that seek to shift their work ever so slightly, at first, to satisfy donors or market whims. Mission drift is akin to moving away from your core business to satisfy a customer. Doing it once might be permissible, but with each additional shift, the nonprofit risks losing itself in the process.

Nonprofits experiencing new growth, site expansion, or service extension are likely good places for corporate career changers. Opportunities exist for entrepreneurial sorts to start up a new nonprofit in a new city, thus combining the start-up energy of a new site with the established playbook of the national office. Further, growth opportunities enable nonprofits to look at how they accomplish their business, allowing for the insertion of best practices from the corporate world where appropriate.

Steady and Stable

Many nonprofits are in a steady and stable mode and remain there for years. Just as nonprofits with histories spanning a hundred years may suddenly find themselves in start-up or transition mode, young nonprofits may, too, find themselves charting a steady and stable course. Steady and stable nonprofits know what they do, and they do it well. They are more interested in perfecting their work and, possibly, sharing best practices among the field or influencing policy, than in pursuing explosive growth. Nonprofits like these have experienced start-up and sometimes transition phases and have mastered their work in one or two cities. Then, 10 to 15 years later, they might suddenly find themselves expanding to 10 or 15 cities at once.

Steady and stable nonprofits spend time perfecting their external work but also looking at internal systems and procedures. The lack of crisis-mode thinking gives them an opportunity to sit back and reflect. Some nonprofits take advantage of this; many do not.

Corporate career changers would be wise to ask hard questions in the interviews and in their networking about how serious the nonprofit is about "fixing what some on staff might think isn't broken." They might also be forewarned that the pace of these organizations will likely be the slowest in the nonprofit sector, and the culture might be the hardest into which a new approach, person, or business background can integrate itself.

In Decline

Nonprofits in decline have either been steady and stable too long, while the market has passed them by, or they got the market wrong and their start-up or growth was a colossal failure. It's not hard to spot a nonprofit in decline. They may have board members who have been around for more than ten years; after five or six, most board members are tapped out of fundraising contacts and intellectual contributions and should move on. They may have a stagnant, non-diversified funding base or, worse yet, a shrinking one. As with any business, reliance on one or two big customers—in the nonprofit sector, donors—is dangerous. For example, an organization may be relying on government funding when a change in the state legislature can easily cut funding by three quarters.

Nonprofits in decline don't necessarily fail. Some get revitalized and enter into start-up or growth mode again. Others must go through a founder transition or a leadership change. Some get a random act of media, the much-coveted notice by Oprah or a feature on the local news that sparks new interest and new funding. As you would size up the prospects of any company for whom you would work, do the same with the nonprofits that interest you. Ask to see a budget. Read the annual report. Determine if there is new thinking, new blood, and new energy or if the nonprofit will be relying chiefly on you to bring those qualities to the table.

A Note on Founder-Run Organizations

Founder-run organizations are an animal all to themselves. Before we get too far, let's make one thing clear: founders are the people who start an organization, but they may also be the ones who get it through a major opportunity, crisis, or collapse. They did not necessarily give birth to the organization, just the organization as you know it today. In response to their energy, the organization becomes a cult of personality, where the staff and board are all working to please the leader regardless of whether or not directives fall in line with the business plan. (For the rest of this section, we will refer to these leaders as "founders.")

Founders have specific character traits. They are charismatic and dynamic; they can talk almost anyone into doing or giving almost anything. They are singularly focused on the mission at hand but wear blinders against anything that might get in their way. Through sheer willpower alone, they often seem to trample roadblocks. They may surround themselves with sycophantic true believers unlikely to play devil's advocate or point out landmines. They are energetic and exuberant, and no one will work harder for a cause than them.

Founders can be enormously exciting to work for, especially when they are in their element. Founders in start-ups or growth-oriented nonprofits can leap light-years ahead of where a more staid manager might take an organization. However, founder types in nonprofits in transition, at a steady and stable point, or in decline can be phenomenally destructive. As in the corporate sector, the nonprofit sector recognizes "founder's syndrome," even if the founder doesn't. No founder wants to stay past their prime, but most simply don't see that it has passed. In fact, staff and board members are often complicit in founder's syndrome, continuing to remain supportive in public even if they have begun snickering in private.

Beware the founder who is still "hiring" board members or participating in all staffing decisions, prizes loyalty above skills, personally holds all close donor relationships, or who seems dismissive of opportunities to change. Make sure to ask about their exit strategy;

Nonprofit Language Clues

Which words does a nonprofit use to describe itself? Its language may give you insight into its lifecycle stage.

Start-up:

- Entrepreneurial

- Adept and agile

- Angel investors

Growth-oriented:

- Scalable program model

- Strategic partnerships

- National model

In transition:

- Re-examination in progress

- Internal assessment and evaluation

- Rebuilding and renewing

Steady and stable:

- Proven program model

- Continuing excellence

In decline:

- Increased turnover

- Homogenous funding base

Founder-run:

- Singular vision

- Driving force

- Staff-driven

most won't have one. Any founder who does is worth entertaining as your next boss.

When founders retire or leave, many organizations go into a tailspin. A personality crisis arises, and a leadership vacuum emerges. Corporate career changers can get caught in this middle of a confused board and a staff fighting to retain their core nonprofit values. Corporate transitioners looking to work for a founder should look to organizations with business savvy and a history of hiring those with corporate experience. Doing so will ensure that they aren't left holding the bag when the executive office empties out.

The lifecycle stage of a nonprofit is one of the most obvious indicators of success for a sector switcher. It is also one aspect of your job search that you can easily control. Forecast your success by discerning the nonprofit's lifecycle stage before it assigns you a desk and prints your business cards. Pay careful attention to the clues found in the job description, the annual report, grant applications, or the interviewing style of your future coworkers. If they are saying one thing but act otherwise, you may have found an organization not quite ready for change. Conversely, if all signs point to progress, proceed knowing that this nonprofit has likely accepted and embraced its future.

An Alternative:
Socially Responsible Businesses

For some, transition is motivated by an overwhelming urge to do good but does not necessarily come with a temperament or skill set that works well in the nonprofit sector. Rest assured that there are still plenty of ways to create social impact, even without compromising your personal economic value or your operating environment comfort level. Consider the socially responsible business as a promising alternative.

Socially responsible businesses give substantial consideration not just to their economic value but to their social value as well. This category does not include corporations that invest large chunks of profits into nonprofits bearing their names; while a noble and much-

Socially Responsible Businesses

There are many socially responsible businesses. Here are just a few examples:

Consumer goods:

- Eileen Fisher

- Procter & Gamble

- The Body Shop

Food:

- Ben & Jerry's

- Newman's Own

- Stonyfield Farms

Personal investing:

- The Calvert Group

- Northstar Asset Management

- Putnam Investments

Service-providing:

- Bright Horizons Family Solutions

- United Parcel Service

- Working Assets

For more companies like these, check out Business for Social Responsibility (www.bsr.org) and Social Venture Network (www.svn.org).

needed endeavor, the Ronald McDonald House does not alone make McDonald's into a socially responsible business. Rather, the "double bottom line," doing what is right even if it means shaving off some profits, makes for corporate social responsibility.

Often, the social value provides great public relations fodder for the business, thus raising the economic value in turn. In addition to the public relations benefit, companies with socially responsible charters also find that they are better able to retain staff, align management and board with shareholders, and create brand loyalty for reasons above and beyond product quality. Some socially responsible businesses were founded on social value principals, while others have recently internalized corporate social responsibility as part of their mission and vision. Prospective sector switchers should see socially responsibly companies as a haven for corporate minds with conscientious hearts.

Conclusion

For every corporate transitioner, there is a job in the nonprofit sector. Finding that job demands a careful review of your priorities and passions, the approach you'd like to take in advancing your chosen cause, and the skills and experience you bring to bear. These past two chapters have taken you through the factors that go into these decisions. Once you have determined where in the sector you want to be, it is important to educate yourself about the special considerations that will face you in your transition. Let's get to those now.

Testimonials from Successful Career Changers:

Malinda Anderson
Vice President of Administration,
Special Olympics Colorado, Denver, Colorado

Having gone back to school after becoming a single parent, Malinda chose a practical major, accounting, through which she could support her family. She got a great job offer from one of the nation's largest accounting firms. "Two weeks into my auditing career," she says, "I realized that I'd made a huge vocational error." Despite being promoted repeatedly, Malinda felt that her work lacked meaning. When one of her clients, a restaurant group in Scottsdale, Arizona, offered her an in-house position, Malinda quickly made the move.

"I was working in their accounting department as a general ledger supervisor and auditor, and I was bored," she says. One day, Malinda approached the chief operations officer and asked what he thought about creating a regional marketing position and hiring her to do it in their Denver, Colorado, cluster market. "In order to be successful in my new job and to get the know the community," she says, "I started volunteering on the funds distribution committee for the United Way as soon as I got to Denver." One of the people she met through her volunteer work was a headhunter who told her about a position at a local but nationally renowned nonprofit Montessori early childhood education agency. "They hired me because I could bring business thinking to their nonprofit organization," she says.

How did Malinda find her current position at the Special Olympics of Colorado?

After 14 years with the Montessori school, Malinda was told by another headhunter about two positions in administration and finance for Special Olympics Colorado. "I'd donated to them for years," she says, "but I was afraid that neither of the positions by themselves would be challenging enough for me." Instead, Malinda approached them about the possibility of combining both positions into one senior level position and leaving some room in the budget to hire a junior staff member for her team. "Nonprofits have got to keep up with the market," she says, "and so taking a more creative look at this position was the right thing for them to do."

What difficulties did encounter Malinda as she made her transition from "Big Accounting" to a small nonprofit?

Malinda was most surprised about the lack of procedures and the lack of administrative controls in the nonprofit sector. "There seemed to be a lack of expertise at the administrative level," she says, "because so many program administrators started off as great front-line program staff and got promoted without the proper administrative training." Likewise, Malinda met many administrators without a program background who didn't understand how to approach problem solving in a way that would resonate with their coworkers. "People in the nonprofit sector aren't driven by the same motives as their corporate counterparts," she says. "They understand that the bottom line is important, but it's only part of the equation. Learning how to talk about numbers in the context of services provided and lives changed is the key to success in the nonprofit sector."

Malinda's Key Lessons Learned:

- ✓ "A good first step is to get involved with United Way or a community board."
- ✓ "Many who wish to transition see marketing and development as logical first steps, and so there is a lot of competition for those jobs. Keep in mind the financial and accounting areas, too."
- ✓ "If you want to succeed in solving problems, be prepared to soften your approach a bit and speak the language of the heart-driven people in the nonprofit sector."

David Orlinoff
Self-Employed Consultant,
Concord Financial Organization, Concord, Massachusetts

"I quit my job as the chief financial officer of a $50 million business at 6:00 p.m. on a Friday night," explains David, "and, according to my wife, it was the first time in three months that I came home standing up straight." Having spent ten years in senior corporate financial positions, David suddenly found himself without work. "As I started thinking about what to do next, I came upon the idea of becoming a 'CFO for hire,' or as one of my friends called it, an RFO, a roving financial officer." With a background in technology, software, and manufacturing, David sought out only corporate clients.

In the spring of 1990, after three years of consulting, David's biggest client hired a permanent financial officer, and for the first time in two years, David opened up the help-wanted section of the newspaper looking for potential consulting opportunities. He saw an ad for Combined Jewish Philanthropies (CJP) and set out to sell himself as a consultant. On meeting CJP's president, he learned that only a full-time job was available, and he decided to accept it when it was offered.

"I had been there less than a month when I realized that the nonprofit world is where I belong," explains David. "There was an understanding of values that went beyond financial incentives." When David found himself at the top of his profession in terms of status and compensation, he headed back into consulting. "In 1996, I hung out my shingle again as a consultant, but this time saying, 'I am an expert in nonprofit management, having worked at one.' Luckily, this strategy worked."

As a consultant, how does David remain connected to the missions of his clients?

"There is a cliché in business that everybody is in sales," explains David, "but in nonprofits, everyone is in fundraising." Regardless of their connection or particular professional specialty, David believes that everyone must act as a representative of the mission of their nonprofit. Further, David understands that a nonprofit's program and fundraising can succeed only if they are intimately intertwined with smart financial management. "The finance staff needs to approach the program and fundraising staff as their customers," he explains. "Internal customer service is essential: it's not that the customer is always right, but the customer at least deserves an explanation."

Why did David go into consulting, and how did he build his practice?

"Consulting gives me the best opportunity to combine my experience and interest in finding new challenges for the benefit of mission-driven organizations." His three dozen clients over the past ten years have ranged from very small community development organizations to larger nonprofits like Oxfam America and the Boston Ballet. Referrals come from business contacts such as lawyers, bankers, and accountants and from satisfied clients. Often David arrives at a nonprofit on short notice to replace a CFO who has left, whether voluntarily or not. "Usually I'm not competing for an engagement directly with another potential consultant," David explains, "Rather, I'm competing with the possibility that the organization will do nothing until it hires a permanent new CFO."

What has made David successful as a consultant?

David combines financial management acumen with the sensibilities of community, mission, and values. "I have learned that nonprofit managers and directors seem to respond to my ability to explain to them in their own vocabulary what they need to know about my area of expertise," he explains. Further, he has truly internalized the structural differences that go beyond the legal form of organization or the bottom line of the organization. "In a nonprofit, since we know that no one owns it, you have to really be sensitive to all of the stakeholders."

David's Key Lessons Learned:

✓ "People looking to transition from industry to nonprofit often act as though their experience automatically qualifies them to work for any nonprofit of their choice. I tell them, 'If you are looking for a job in the nonprofit world, don't start off by saying you want to give something back. If you are looking to give something back, write a check. Instead, approach your target nonprofit by telling them why they need you, not why you need them.'"

✓ "It is almost always harder to manage in the nonprofit sector because of limitations on resources and the multiple accountabilities. But, if you have a tolerance for ambiguity—which a lot financial people don't have—you'll find managing in the nonprofit sector much more gratifying than managing in the corporate sector."

✓ "If you want to go into consulting, you really need to believe in it. Otherwise, you are just a person in between jobs, and you and the world will see you that way. For me, the watershed, psychologically validating event was the first time I had two clients at the same time.

CHAPTER 4:

Myth Busters for the Career Changer

The nonprofit sector of today is home to a great variety of organizations; running the gamut from social workers to social entrepreneurs, there is a place in the nonprofit sector for everyone. But what about you, the corporate transitioner? Where do you belong? What about the myths you've heard as you've told friends about your job search? What do you need to know, and how can you combat the stereotypes you will face? And, finally, the $64,000 question: what will it mean, financially, for you to make this move?

This chapter will discuss and dismiss ten widely held myths about the nonprofit sector. While one of those myths—that nonprofit employees are paid starvation wages—is blatantly false, there is a significant compensation gap. This chapter will help you consider the financial implications of your new career. We'll also discuss the common stereotypes that may be assigned to you, your career path, and your personal motivations and ways you can dispel them. Lastly, we'll review different personalities of nonprofits to determine which type is right for you and your corporate background, pointing out those types of nonprofits that make for an easier career change.

Ten Myths about Working in the Nonprofit Sector

Myths about nonprofits abound. You may have heard a few from your friends and colleagues as you've told them about your nonprofit search:

- "You've turned into a do-gooder."
- "You've gone soft."
- "You will decimate your savings account."
- "If you want to work less, you should just retire."

In fact, none of these statements could be further from the truth. Every day, people come to work in the nonprofit sector because they have decided to do something bigger than themselves, to set in motion events that will solve a problem plaguing society, or to answer a call that they have felt inside for some time. Others come to the sector because they are looking for a more flexible schedule, because they have made their money and want to give back, or because they are looking for an entirely new challenge. Figure D lays out the advantages—and disadvantages—of transitioning to the nonprofit sector.

Like the variety of people looking to join the nonprofit sector, the sector itself is full of differences. Yet some myths persist about the sector as a whole.

Myth #1: You Have to Starve to Work in the Nonprofit Sector

The fattest line on most nonprofits' budgets is payroll and benefits, yet nonprofit organizations remain infamous for underpaying talent. There is no disputing the fact that nonprofits generally pay far less than their corporate counterparts for the same level of talent. This is not something nonprofits choose to do; it is something they are forced to do. Often, their funders demand it, expecting that the vast majority of any donation will address service needs in the field, not overhead at the home office.

Figure D. Advantages and Disadvantages for Transitioners:

Advantages	Disadvantages
• Your work will be rewarding. You will become rich in spirit, feeling purposeful in every action and able to point to change made as a result.	• You may not be rewarded as highly for your work. You are unlikely to become rich in dollars. While the nonprofit sector has become more competitive, salaries still lag behind those offered in the corporate sector.
• You will be asked to take on responsibility for a broad portfolio of work and will amaze yourself while doing what you thought you could never accomplish.	• You will be asked to do more with less training and fewer resources and will have to learn along the way.
• You will be able to advance your career easily, because nonprofits often have opportunities to capture or leadership vacuums to fill.	• Your career advancement may not come in a strategic, linear fashion, nor will it come with training for the next level of work.
• Opportunities to move within the sector abound, and increases in responsibility, pay, and authority can come quickly.	• Smaller nonprofits often have opportunity ceilings when long-standing leadership has no plans to move on. Advancement often comes by moving into larger organizations.
• The work environment will be positive, filled with people who share with you a higher calling around a specific mission area.	• A singular focus on a mission area can sometimes hamper progress toward a goal.
• Greater acceptance of and flexibility around lifestyle changes allows for those with nontraditional availability to contribute meaningfully.	• Bending too far to accommodate some staff can overextend others, leading to frustration and burnout.
• Everyone gets a vote. By listening to opinions from a large and diverse group of stakeholders, nonprofits often make unexpected and wiser choices.	• Everyone gets a vote. Meetings can sometimes be endless, opinions may be valued disproportionately to their merit, and staff can get disheartened.

The most difficult funding a nonprofit can secure is funding for general operating costs, including salaries. Funders want to say that their money went to hepatitis vaccinations for 600 infants, books for 100 students, or meals delivered to 50 elderly shut-ins. No one wants to boast to their friends or their board of directors that they gave $50,000 to the Boys and Girls Clubs of Atlanta to pay half the salary of one third of the IT department. It's not sexy, although without that half salary for a third of the IT department, not one child in Atlanta would get the mentoring services that those "sexier" donations fund. At the end of the day, dollars are dollars to a nonprofit regardless of how they are earmarked; the earmarking just makes for harder accounting, which, ironically, costs the nonprofits more general operating dollars in the end. If you want to get really righteously indignant about this, check out Dan Pallotta's TED talk on the subject of overhead and compensation (*http://on.ted.com/Pallotta*).

However, while it is true that most nonprofits are looking for $300,000 of talent for only $100,000 a year, nonprofit salaries are becoming more and more competitive. Funders are becoming increasingly sophisticated and some have begun to use a venture philanthropy approach, rewarding high-functioning nonprofits with general (i.e., unrestricted) funds for purposes such as attracting great talent. Such funding has allowed nonprofits to pay more competitive wages for staff with a broader set of skills, like you and your fellow corporate expats.

In addition, some nonprofits pay better than others. Organizations fighting for civil rights, human rights, women's rights, or animal rights tend to pay towards the lower end of the spectrum. In fact, it's not uncommon to find nonprofits that fight against poverty wages paying their own employees impossibly low salaries. Smaller organizations that have been run by the same person for long periods of time are less likely to have faced a competitive analysis of their wages. As such, they may not be paying current market value for their people. Conversely, nonprofits with high staff turnover have spent a great deal of time and effort negotiating job offers and better understand the wages they need to pay.

Research institutions, colleges and universities, think and action tanks, consulting firms, and foundations, for example, tend to pay towards the top of the nonprofit sector and also have more comprehensive benefits packages. Simply put: the closer you are to touching the people in need, the less you'll likely make.

Nonprofit Salaries

In 2012, the leadership of some of the nation's largest nonprofits made salaries that, while likely far below what they would have made in the corporate sector, were still quite attractive. According to reports filed by each organization with the IRS, following are the annual salaries for 2012:

Surgeon-in-Chief
Children's Hospital Medical Center, Cincinnati, Ohio   **$1,631,748**

President
John F. Kennedy Center for Performing Arts, Washington, D.C.   **$1,450,283**

President
Yale University, New Haven, Connecticut   **$1,356,767**

President
J. Paul Getty Trust, Los Angeles, California   **$970,236**

President, *Global Health*,
Bill and Melinda Gates Foundation, Seattle, Washington   **$883,867**

Chief Operating Officer
Public Broadcasting System Foundation, Alexandria, Virginia   **$498,900**

President
United Negro College Fund, Fairfax, Virginia   **$458,497**

Chief Executive Officer
Ducks Unlimited, Memphis, Tennessee   **$409,036**

Chief of Regional Growth
Special Olympics, Washington, D.C.   **$251,927**

Myth #2: Working in the Nonprofit Sector Will Deplete Your Retirement

Years ago, nonprofits were lucky to be able to pay the wages of their employees. Nowadays, nonprofits know that to hire and retain excellent staff, they must offer competitive benefits packages as well. Nonprofit employees have come to expect retirement contributions, relocation reimbursement, flexible work schedules, health and dental insurance, life and disability insurance, and generous vacation plans. More and more nonprofits extend these benefits to same-sex or other domestic partners.

Nonprofits have—from both necessity and desire—become more creative in the benefits they offer. Instead of offering high salaries, some nonprofits offer inflated titles. You can't discount the feelings of a 30-year-old who is becoming senior vice president of operations after five long years as an anonymous staff associate in a large corporation. Some nonprofits have gone further, offering additional vacation time or a laptop to take home, knowing that employees are there because they care deeply about the work and (frankly) are not likely to take the additional vacation, or are likely to put in time on nights and weekends. Finally, some nonprofits have become quite inventive, allowing their staffs to bring their pets to work or using some of their in-kind donations, like theatre tickets, restaurant gift certificates, or gym memberships, as performance rewards for high-achieving staff.

Finally, nonprofit work is steeped in nonmonetary benefits as well. Studies have shown that nonprofit workers have the healthiest morale compared to those in the government or private sectors. They have the easiest time connecting their day-to-day tasks with the overall mission of the organization and, thus, their specific contribution to society. Further, they feel that they have a greater opportunity to learn new skills, take on larger levels of responsibility, and be respected by society at large for their contributions to the world.

Myth #3: Money Is Evil

If nonprofits pay living wages and decent benefits, then surely nonprofit employees must feel some guilt about earning money, right? Wrong! Money is not considered an evil in the nonprofit sector. In fact, nonprofits love money just like corporations; it's just that they get the money as a reward for different achievements and from different sources. Long gone are the times when people in nonprofits apologized for coming from money, making money, or enjoying the spoils of having money. Still, a connection to the mission of a nonprofit is more important than a connection to money. In other words, you will be judged by your nonprofit peers more closely by what is in your heart than what is in your wallet.

Nonprofits are becoming increasingly sophisticated about their approach toward money. Not only do nonprofits embrace those with money as donors—not much has changed on that front—but they now embrace those who have money as employees as well. Nonprofits are increasingly adding revenue-generating projects to their portfolio of activities and expecting higher rates of returns on investment of time, energy, money, and other resources. Doing so means that those from the corporate sector are more and more attractive to nonprofits going forward.

Myth #4: All Nonprofit Employees Are Saints

One of the biggest fallacies spun by those in the corporate sector about people in the nonprofit sector is that everyone in the sector is a good-doing do-gooder. Just because people work for good doesn't always make them good people. The same ladder climbing, social scheming, and personal selfishness exists in the sector of forgiveness and grace as it does everywhere else in the world. Foibles and quirks are endemic to human nature, regardless of the sector. While a nonprofit might hold its weekly staff meeting seated in a circle, you are unlikely to find a campfire in the center or hand-holding revelers breaking out in choruses of "Kumbayah."

Overgeneralizing the nonprofit sector into a place where idealists earn poverty wages to fight injustices for every member of society, changing the world one hot lunch at a time, or protecting every living creature no matter the cost is simply that—an overgeneralization. Certainly those people exist, and in much larger numbers in the nonprofit sector than anywhere else, but they aren't the dominant force. Nonprofit sector employees are just like you: focused on working towards a particular goal with both career advancement and competitive salaries in mind. It's just that the goal is different: instead of trying to get themselves a bigger slice of the pie, they are trying to make the pie bigger for all.

Myth #5: Nonprofits Are Lucky to Employ Whomever They Can Find

Many corporate career changers believe that the passion they hold for the nonprofit's cause is enough to make them an attractive candidate for employment. The truth is that passion helps, but it isn't the whole picture. Consider that nonprofits have limited amounts of money for hiring and retaining staff, and remember that poor hiring choices cost the nonprofit more money than hiring no one at all. Knowing this, nonprofits can and will be picky about whom they choose to employ.

Nonprofits will not hire you if you don't hold the requisite skills and experience for you to hit the ball out of the park as you walk in the door. That being said, you'll also need the passion for the cause or a track record of volunteering for some mission-driven organization. Even if you haven't volunteered for a particular cause, a history of volunteering anywhere shows a side of you that is attractive to nonprofits.

Myth #6: Working in Nonprofits Is Not Challenging

Ask anyone in a nonprofit if their work is easy, and they will likely laugh at you—and for good reason. Not only is the work difficult, but also many would argue that it is much more difficult than working in the corporate sector. Employees in nonprofit organizations are often asked to do more with less, in shorter periods of time, while considering more opinions and keeping more people happy than do their corporate counterparts. The results of this hard work are often intangible; it's harder to measure how much closer to a cure for breast cancer one got today than, say, how many miles of PVC pipe you sold. Similarly, the goals are often unattainable; it's difficult to get up every day and end world hunger or clean the planet's oceans. Simply put, the need never ends, so the job never ends.

If you are looking to do a little good work, take a little time to relax, and feel as though you are making a contribution to society, make your next vacation an "alternate vacation," one that you spend contributing your time in service to a cause about which you care deeply. Volunteer. Make a donation. Find someone and help them. If you are looking to create systemic change in a full-time capacity, know that the work will be hard but likely the most rewarding work you have ever done. That old Peace Corps slogan is brilliant: working in the nonprofit sector will be "the toughest job you'll ever love."

Myth #7: Nonprofits Are All Flat, Nonhierarchical Places

Culture shock for sector switchers comes in many forms, from salary discrepancies to the lack of updated technology. The biggest culture shock, however, comes for those expecting the direct line of authority they found in the corporate sector. Many small nonprofits are flat organizations, where the intern has as much opportunity to voice opinions and affect change as the senior vice president. In some of the older, more staid nonprofits, this can be maddening. It impedes progress, slows decision-making, and reduces a nonprofit's ability to affect change. It's a heck of a good strategy for increasing staff morale at the lowest levels, though, where staff is paid next to nothing and the work can be tedious.

However, there is no one organizational chart for all nonprofits. Some are more hierarchical than others. In today's nonprofit world, it is easier to find nonprofits that have adopted the latest in management techniques. In fact, as more and more Fortune 500 executives are leaving the corporate sector for new, fulfilling careers in the nonprofit sector, they are taking their expertise with them and molding their management practices to drive success in the nonprofit sector. Career changers who choose the right nonprofits can find not only fulfilling work environments with familiar structures but also opportunities to create real change in issues close to their hearts.

Myth #8: Nonprofit Jobs Are Secure

Some nonprofits—the United Way, Kiwanis International, and the Girl Scouts, just to name a few—have been around for ages. These community stalwarts are driven by volunteers and have likely been run by just a handful of leaders during their long existences. Most jobs in the nonprofit sector, though, can be insecure and depend highly on the whim of a funder or two. Remember that just because the issue is well funded now doesn't mean it will always be.

Take, for example, nonprofits that focus on issues related to AIDS/HIV. It was all the rage to fund AIDS research in the 1980s and 1990s; everyone was looking for a cure. However, once scientists came up with drug cocktails that extended the life of those living with HIV and AIDS, the river of funding slowed to a trickle. AIDS nonprofits found that the demand was not for a cure, despite the fact that one has yet to be found, but for services that would increase the life expectancy and quality of those living with the disease. Cure-focused nonprofits were forced to shut down or change their missions to align with the desires of funders.

Myth #9: Nonprofit Managers Know How to Manage

Nonprofits can't offer the same professional development as their corporate competitors. This isn't to say that nonprofits don't care about their people. They do, in fact, care deeply about their people; they just have odd ways of showing it. It's not typical in the nonprofit sector for there to be any purposeful focus placed on internal management development, successor grooming, or skills training. It is much more haphazard or sporadic than in the corporate sector. There are two reasons for this.

First, many founding executive directors are in those roles because they were exceptionally good at the front-line, direct service work of the nonprofit sector. Someone noticed and gave them some money to expand and do more, and the next thing they knew, they were sitting on top of a ten-site, multimillion dollar change agent that was a management catastrophe on the inside. These founders have the best of intentions but still a singular vision for the communities they serve. At the same time, they have gotten to where they are because of this vision. They are unlikely to have stopped along the way for management training or reflective thinking about building staff or grooming successors. Because of this, while they may deeply desire a well-oiled management team that employs sound business practices and effective staff development; they simply may not know how to make it a reality.

Second, resources of nonprofits are constrained. If faced with the choice of spending money on the guaranteed, quick return of more services to the field or on the uncertainty of training for a staff member

> **McKinsey surveyed 200 nonprofit CEOs** in November 2014 and found that 59 percent of them believed that the lack of an effective senior team undermines the effectiveness of the organization and the sector as a whole.
>
> http://www.mckinsey.com/insights/social_sector/what_social_sector_leaders_need_to_succeed?cid=other-eml-alt-mip-mck-oth-1411

who may or may not blossom and may or may not remain with the organization long-term, most managers would choose the former rather than the latter. Most nonprofits aren't large enough to offer a specific career path and an obvious "next step" internally, so with many staff members looking outside for their next opportunity, allocating resources to training becomes less attractive. A recent survey noted that nearly 70 percent of nonprofits lack succession plans.[21]

21. "What Social Sector Leaders Need to Succeed: Chronic underinvestment is placing increasing demands on social-sector leaders. New research suggests ways they can meet the leadership challenge. "Laura Callanan, Nora Gardner, Lenny Mendonca, and Doug Scott, November 2014,_http://www.mckinsey.com/insights/social_sector/what_social_sector_leaders_need_to_succeed?cid=other-eml-alt-mip-mck-oth-1411.

Nonprofit employees must take an active role in their professional development, seeking out mentors and training opportunities on their own and building a case to their management about why funds should be expended for training. The odds are that a good case will go far.

Myth #10: A Nonprofit Is a Nonprofit Is a Nonprofit

Nonprofit organizations are as different from one another as corporate companies. Just as you would never compare Xerox Global to your local neighborhood copy shop, you shouldn't assume that the Girl Scouts of America is the same as Girls Scouts of Poughkeepsie or any other girls-mentoring organization. Beyond the obvious differences of mission and focus, key differences in nonprofits include size, age, outlook, business model, and bylaws.

Volunteering for a nonprofit will give you a good sense of the style of that particular organization. Volunteering for two organizations will allow you to start comparing differences. Each is like a piece of a patchwork quilt. Only once you've started to see the vast array of nonprofits can you begin to understand the beauty and complexity of the quilt as a whole.

Dealing with the Financial Implications of a Nonprofit Salary

If you are considering a move into the nonprofit sector, you have likely already accepted the fact that you will make less—perhaps a lot less—than you are currently making in your corporate career. There is a reason they call it "nonprofit" after all. Your nonprofit salary might be as little as 40 percent of your corporate equivalent, but it doesn't have to be. Still, let's consider some ways to deal with the financial implications of your nonprofit salary.

Determine Your Readiness Factor

Are you an empty nester with the house paid off and the children out of school? Are you a single professional with only a cat to concern you? Or is college tuition for three kids looming? Has your company gone public, yielding a return greater than expected? Determining your personal financial situation will allow you to decide whether you can afford to consider the nonprofit sector.

All of that being said, many corporate employees find themselves in nonprofit job interviews because they simply cannot afford not to make this change. Something has happened to them, or to the world in general, that has set off a series of events leading them to feel that things must change and that they must be the one to make this change happen. For these individuals, money isn't a question.

Learn to Value the Intangibles

Nonprofit jobs come with many nonmonetary rewards. There is simply no direct correlation, as in the corporate sector, between the salary you earn and the value you deliver to society. Don't focus on the paycheck—look around at the rest of the picture. You have saved the spotted owls. You have taught a child to read. You have reduced hunger.

Adding up the intangible benefits of working in a nonprofit will make you feel, in the words of Lou Gehrig, like "the luckiest [wo]man on the face of the Earth." This can sometimes be a difficult task, given that needs always outweigh resources, regardless of the nonprofit.

Change Your Lifestyle

If you are ready to make the move to the nonprofit sector but are not in a financial position to do so, consider scaling down your expenses and lifestyle. Perhaps the cause you hold dear is more important that those extra nights out at fancy restaurants or another designer handbag. Consider holding back any extra expenses for a few months to determine whether the sacrifice both gets you to where you need to be financially and is palatable for you in the long term. If not, you will come to resent your nonprofit's cause and its staff, souring you on the opportunity to transition later in your career, when you may have saved up enough money or emptied your nest.

Don't Settle for Less

Try to find a job that pays towards the upper end of the nonprofit spectrum. Don't settle for less money than you could comfortably afford to make. Consider the new social venture movement in the nonprofit sector or the for-profit ventures of nonprofits that fund their work. Or look into socially responsible businesses as a way to make the move into the nonprofit sector in stages. Socially responsible businesses are for-profit businesses that demonstrate respect for ethical values, people, communities, and the environment. And, since these businesses are for-profit entities, you might temporarily soothe your need to do better by the world while not doing too poorly by your bank account.

Rethink Your Value

An unfortunate byproduct of a market-driven economy is that we live in a society where self-value is often derived from what someone else thinks we should earn. Salary equals worthiness, right? Not so in the nonprofit sector. You need to separate your own self-value from the amount of zeroes printed on your paycheck. Agonizing over the difference in corporate valuation and nonprofit valuation will get you nowhere. Instead, look at what you are earning compared to others performing similar tasks in the nonprofit sector. With all the talent and skills you are bringing along, you may find that you are, in fact, "paid" pretty well.

Think Ahead

Start thinking now about your cash-flow situation. When will your financial situation allow you to make this move? What do you really need to earn? What do you really want to earn? How much do you need to put away each month now to accept a lower salary later? Answering these questions will enable you to plan your nonprofit career change with increased comfort.

Remember that you still have options if your nonprofit dream job comes with a less than dreamy, but still potentially palatable, salary. To make this move a reality, try to negotiate the total package, not just the annual compensation.

Tie Salary Increases to Achievements

When interviewing, ask if the job has a growth track. If it does, you may be able to accept a lower salary for six months while working toward the achievement of very specific benchmarks of success. Ask your hiring manager to write into your offer letter that you will sit down with your future boss after you have been on the job for six weeks to determine what you expect to achieve by the 6-, 12-, 18-, and 24-month anniversaries of your hire. Enlist a partnership with the nonprofit such that your earnings will rise as the nonprofit grows. Tying your salary to its overall growth shouldn't be hard for the nonprofit to imagine.

The Commission Fallacy

It is taboo for development professionals to earn a certain percentage of the money they raise. A better benchmark of success would be an increase in the organization's overall budget, numbers of new donors, or scale of services rendered. Ask for scheduled reviews of performance that link pay raises to specific goals met.

Just Say No

If you will be spending your work hours worrying about how to pay your bills, you won't be much use to a nonprofit. When a job offer is made that is too low for you to accept, call your interviewer and talk to them openly about how much you would love to accept the job if only it were just a little more financially viable for you. They may be able to pull some strings internally or bend a few rules to increase a benefits package. Even if they can't, you have made a valuable connection when, later, you go back to this or another nonprofit organization. Saying no to an unattractive job offer puts you both in a better financial position in the long run and makes you more attractive to the nonprofit should you decide later that you can afford the reduced salary. In the meantime, you can cement your relationship with them and prove your value by showing your stuff as a volunteer.

Common Stereotypes about Corporate Job Candidates

There is no doubt that the hiring manager or headhunter looking at your résumé has seen many corporate applicants in the past. There is also no doubt, unfortunately, the manager has had bad experiences with some of them, just as he certainly had with nonprofit candidates. Most corporate career changers come to the nonprofit sector with any one of a number of expectations, and because of this, your application may be stereotyped.

Some of the most common stereotypes include the following:

- "You are used to getting things done by delegating work to the many support staff you have had at your disposal."

- "You expect that you will be rewarded handsomely for your work and will have plenty of resources to get the job done."

- "The impact of your work on the bottom line is the only appropriate gauge of success."

- "You think that because you have raised investment money, you will easily be able to raise nonprofit funds."

- "You are looking to step out of the rat race, slow down, and work less hard."

- "You think that nonprofits would run better if only they ran just like corporations."

- "You will change the culture of the nonprofit by imprinting your corporate stamp everywhere."

- "You value money more than people and make only rational, not emotional, decisions."

- "You are not succeeding in your corporate work and think the nonprofit sector will be easier."
- "If you really cared so deeply about the mission, you wouldn't have sold out to the corporate sector so many years ago."

Now, before you gnash your teeth in anger, remember that the corporate sector holds plenty of mistaken opinions about the nonprofit sector—including the ten myths we discussed earlier in this chapter—as well. Be prepared for your interviewer to hold one or more (or even all) of these stereotypes. You can correct them. For example, the cover letter is a great place to discuss how you have sent your children to college and are more financially able to make the sacrifices necessary to give back to your community. Or use your résumé to list the volunteer work you've done throughout the years to allay concerns that you don't care about people. Networking is another chance for you to learn about and discuss how work in the nonprofit sector is different, proving that your expectations are aligned with reality. Let's look at these stereotypes one by one, examining them and developing strategic responses.

"You are used to getting things done by delegating work to the many support staff you have had at your disposal."

Expect to be asked about support staff in your interviews or, better yet, beat your interviewer to the punch and tell stories about how you single-handedly swept in and saved the day, especially if it was a task that an underling might have normally done. Avoid stories that involve your assistant making all the arrangements for a meeting, even if that has happened. Remind your interviewer about how your corporation had to manage with less than expected at times and about the role you played in still getting to success.

"You expect that you will be rewarded handsomely for your work and will have plenty of resources to get the job done."

Avoid asking questions about expense accounts and budgets for less than urgent needs. Assume that there is no such money, but be prepared to make a case for what you need once on board. Tell stories about how you strategically reassigned resources or people to get the job done, and done right. Finally, use your cover letter to communicate that you understand that pay in the nonprofit sector differs considerably from that of the corporate sector, and that salary, while important, isn't critical. Indicate that you are open to discussions, and do your homework before you begin any discussion.

"The impact of your work on the bottom line is the only appropriate gauge of success."

Nonprofits use all sorts of indicators to determine success, only few of which are the numbers at the bottom of the budget. Yet it is hard for some career changers to wrap their minds around these softer benchmarks. Nothing is better here than telling a story about how you chose to do the non-profitable, unpopular thing and how the company benefited and learned from it in the end. This proves you to be a change agent unafraid of making waves when doing the right thing is at stake. Nonprofits adore people like this.

"You think that because you have raised investment money, you will easily be able to raise nonprofit funds."

Raising money in either the corporate or the nonprofit sector is both an art and a science. Many corporate candidates come to nonprofit development job assuming that raising money is raising money, regardless of the sector. It isn't. Your nonprofit donors are not going to see the corporate equivalent of a return on investment, unless their bank cashes in good karma for groceries and rent. That being said, people donate to nonprofits for a variety of reasons: tax incentives, business development, community connection, and that good old karma, to name but a few.

Having raised significant money in the corporate sector may not guarantee that you'll be successful raising money in the nonprofit sector, but it may mean that you have some of the requisite arrows in your quiver to get started. Take care to point out what skills you have used in the corporate sector and how they might help you do the same in the nonprofit sector. Just be careful not to assume for your interviewer that all those skills will equal success anywhere. If you lay out the argument well enough, they will get there on their own.

"You are looking to step out of the rat race, slow down, and work less hard."

If your motivation for transitioning to the nonprofit sector is unclear, your interviewer may be concerned that you are switching sectors merely as a way of slowing down. If you are a sector switcher late in your career, you may be viewed as someone looking for an off-ramp from the career highway. Counterbalance this view by presenting an active résumé that highlights tangible results and a cover letter describing what about this nonprofit at this time excites you. Convince the nonprofit that you are energized and excited by a career shift.

"You think that nonprofits would run better if only they ran just like corporations."

Want to really tick off a nonprofit professional? Insist that running their nonprofit like a corporation would solve all their woes. For some, this may be the truth. For others, it's the farthest thing from it. More likely, nonprofits and corporations could each learn something from the other. Propose your solutions judiciously, biting off a little at a time, until you know more.

"You are going to change the culture of the nonprofit by imprinting your corporate stamp everywhere."

One of the biggest fears held by nonprofits it that the corporate job seeker won't assimilate to the nonprofit, but expect the nonprofit to assimilate to him. Highlight your flexibility and willingness to adapt. Come armed with stories about how, in your corporate life, you changed your approach in light of new people, new information, or new opportunities. Don't be afraid to show your softer side.

"You value money more than people and make only rational, not emotional, decisions."

Nonprofits are filled with quirky people, most of whom are more tied to the mission of the organization than their paycheck. Because of this, battles sometimes erupt over illogical things. Being able to diffuse tension while holding high the morale of the team is a key skill. Find ways to weave a track record of this into the stories you tell, but be careful not to malign any of the players, lest you seem callous and uncaring. Nonprofits believe that everyone has value; the more you actively appreciate that fact, the more likely it is that you will be seen as being an effective nonprofit manager.

"You are not succeeding in your corporate work and think the nonprofit sector will be easier."

A common mistake made by nonprofit managers is thinking that the only reason someone would enter the nonprofit sector in midcareer is because their corporate career isn't going as planned. Life-altering crises, world events, or personal developments are easily identified entrance points for some candidates, but others just wake up one day and realize that they should be somewhere else doing something else. Use your résumé and cover letter to detail professional success as well as your reasons for making the move at this time.

"If you really cared so deeply about the mission, you wouldn't have sold out to the corporate sector so many years ago."

We all are forced to live with economic reality. Sadly, the mortgage company won't give us back any points for helping the homeless, nor will the supermarket comp us groceries for feeding the poor. Working for the private sector is not and was not a sin, and you should be proud of the work that you did there. It has prepared you for the nonprofit sector in ways that will benefit the nonprofit for which you ultimately work. Yet a nonprofit hiring manager may not see it that way and might need some additional stroking. Take care to craft your story, your "Aha!" moment, when you discovered that you were unfulfilled by the pursuit of money, as it were, and wanted to chase this cause. Nonprofits love to hear about corporate denizens who wake up one day and realize that they want to do more meaningful work. If you wear your heart on your sleeve, the nonprofit sector will applaud your fashion sense.

Finding a Nonprofit That Is Right for You

Combating these myths and dealing with the financial implications of transition can be complicated. Yet these complications can be alleviated by choosing the right nonprofit through which to advance your career. Given that your first nonprofit job will likely not be your last, remember that your second job in the nonprofit sector will be easier to come by once you've had an initial success. Therefore, in thinking about your first nonprofit, consider one that is friendly to those seeking a career change and allows you the greatest chance of a smooth transition and, ultimately, a better nonprofit career trajectory.

"Friendly" Nonprofits for Career Changers

Corporate job seekers tend to be most successful in nonprofits that have already adopted business practices into their daily work. These nonprofits use words like *entrepreneurial* and *cutting-edge* to describe themselves, and they use best practices from the corporate sector to impact their missions. They actively recruit change agents for whom failure to achieve goals is not an option. In the funding hunt, these nonprofits look at traditional types of funding such as government and foundation grants, individuals donors, and special events, but they also seek out new and inventive models of revenue generation, such as corporate subsidiaries or fee-for-service work to underwrite nonprofit operations.

Corporate job seekers can also be successful in organizations that are standing on the precipice of great change. Nonprofits find themselves ready to (or forced to) change at key moments, such as when the interests of funders shift, an unexpected opportunity arises, or a crisis occurs. Whether demanded by their funders, their constituents, or their internal staff, these nonprofits often take this opportunity to examine what they have been doing—and with what kinds of talent—and make adjustments to the way they fulfill their mission. This moment strikes all nonprofits eventually, and when it does, these organizations open themselves to new ways of thinking, creative solutions, and previously untapped skill sets.

Nonprofits Career Changers Should Avoid

Beware the organization that wants to be an entrepreneurial, cutting-edge, business practice-utilizing nonprofit of the future if they aren't already one now. It is very much in vogue today—as demanded by the changing landscape of philanthropy—to want to apply the best practices of business to nonprofits. But it doesn't always work, sometimes because the people involved are incapable or not truly sold on the idea or, more often, business practices simply cannot be applied successfully to the nonprofit in question. Many sector switchers fail because they believe the words of the staff and board that change is afoot, but when push comes to shove, leadership gets cold feet and backs out. It is all well and good to try to tackle this challenge as your second nonprofit job, but make sure that your first is a slam dunk before getting more adventurous, lest the blame for the nonprofit's failure be laid at your feet, labeling you as incapable of making the transition out of corporate work.

Key Words to Look for in Nonprofit Descriptions

How does a nonprofit describe itself? The words it chooses may tell you a great deal about the type of nonprofit it is and what it will be like as a work environment. Here are some verbal cues to listen for:

- **Start-up mode.** Nonprofits in start-up mode operate similarly to corporations in start-up mode. When they are just getting going, they have little definition in their culture and processes, and few expectations exist about the personalities or employees who can fulfill their mission.

- **Entrepreneurial approach.** The nonprofit sees itself as opportunistic, and its leadership is interested in surrounding itself with others of a similar stripe.

- **Crisis point.** The nonprofit is at a crisis point because of funding, politics, or leadership. When nonprofits are faced with an urgent problem, they look to people unlike those currently on staff.

- **Turnaround situation.** The nonprofit is in need of a turnaround. What has worked in the past no longer works, and without change, the organization will die.

- **Social venture, social innovator, fee-for-service, or revenue generation.** The nonprofit includes a social venture component or other corporate venture within its business model, which is used to fund its nonprofit operations.

- **Opportunity for change.** The nonprofit is standing on the precipice of major growth because of a large and unexpected grant, uninvited media attention, or other life-altering event. To go to scale, the nonprofit must look to those in the private sector who have done this in the past.

Corporate job seekers are least likely to be successful when moving into a small, grassroots, hands-on, direct service position, regardless of the approach or overall business model of the nonprofit. Most former corporate employees tend to be frustrated with the slower pace of change when faced with individual nonprofit constituents and find themselves much more satisfied when they can effect change with larger levels of impact. For this reason, most sector switchers tend to look for roles in senior management rather than in front-line service delivery.

Conclusion

Like most myths, the ones about the nonprofit sector are based more on prejudice that fact. The nonprofit sector of today hardly resembles the nonprofit sector of 5, 10, or 15 years ago. In fact, it barely resembles the nonprofit sector of last year. With each day, the sector becomes savvier and more competitive, and this trend benefits you as a nonprofit job seeker.

Come to the nonprofit sector fully aware of the advantages and disadvantages of what working in it will mean for you personally, professionally, and financially. Like your job in the corporate sector, there will be trade-offs, but with the proper choice of nonprofit and role, the fulfillment you feel at the end of each day will outweigh whatever burdens this career change may bring.

Choose the right type of nonprofit for your corporate background. The more experience the nonprofit has had with business practices or businesspeople, the more likely you will succeed right away and the more enjoyable your work will be. Now that you're acquainted with the nonprofit sector and the types of nonprofits for which you would like to work, let's get ready to start your job search.

Testimonials from Successful Career Changers:

Yutaka Tamura
Founder and Executive Director,
Excel Academy Charter School, Boston, Massachusetts

Yutaka was on the traditional consulting track. He had completed a corporate internship during his undergraduate years and, upon graduating, had landed a job at a prestigious firm in Boston. Yet after fighting to achieve his quantitative bearings and then being promoted twice in two years for his exceptional work, he found himself unhappy. "I finally achieved the level of basic technical skills needed to no longer be the person slaving away at the computer over data analysis," he says, "but I didn't feel personally connected to the work."

The education sector was always an interest of Yutaka's, so he began looking into positions in education both in the nonprofit and the corporate sectors. "Nonprofit or corporate, it didn't matter to me," he says, "Good practice is good practice wherever you are." Yutaka took a couple of positions with growing corporate companies that provided educational services to youth, always with the plan to go to business school. His ultimate goal was to build an educational organization of his own. With his business school acceptance in hand and his deposit paid for Harvard for the fall of 2000, Yutaka's road took another turn.

Why did Yutaka turn down Harvard Business School twice?

Throughout his various jobs, Yutaka was able to interact with the founders of some of the nation's leading education nonprofits and corporations. He learned from them that he needed something he couldn't get in business school. "It was a turning point for me," he says, "to have met these entrepreneurs who were doing what I wanted to do, and finding out that either they were happy to have had operational experience or that they wished they had."

Having been accepted to Harvard Business School (HBS), Yutaka applied at the last minute to a suburban private school and was offered a job as a teacher, so he declined admission to Harvard. Soon after beginning his teaching career, he applied and was accepted again to HBS, and he also applied to the Harvard Graduate School of Education. However, when the dean of students at his private school took a sabbatical, Yutaka accepted the interim dean position and declined his Harvard acceptances once more.

When he realized that private suburban education wasn't his passion, he once again applied to HBS, but this time he didn't get in.

How did Yutaka start his charter school?

A former colleague of his, who was attending HBS at the time, told Yutaka about Building Excellent Schools, a nonprofit that was coming to campus to recruit HBS grads to join a fellowship program and start charter schools. Four years later, as a graduate of the second class of the Building Excellent Schools Fellowship Program, Yutaka now runs one of the most successful schools in Massachusetts.

How did Yutaka prepare for the financial implications of his transition into the nonprofit sector?

Yutaka had saved some money, and he moved somewhere with a lower cost of living. "My rent when I was teaching was $100 less than what I paid for my parking spot in Manhattan," he says. Psychologically, though, Yutaka was following his real passion: education. "Ultimately, we are in a capital society," he says. "If this charter school was a $2 million Internet company that was at the top of its peer group, as we are today, I would be in a position to earn great sums of money. Yet I have worked for four years, never taken a week's vacation, and stand to gain very little financially from this endeavor. On the other hand, I have the opportunity to work on behalf of low-income, urban students who otherwise might not have the ability to get a college-preparatory education and put them squarely on the path to college, enabling them to ultimately change their socioeconomic status." Clearly, intrinsic rewards outweighed extrinsic costs for Yutaka.

Yutaka's Key Lessons Learned:

- ✓ "Go study the people who are the best at doing what you want to do. Learn from their lessons."
- ✓ "If you are motivated and if you do good work, most reasonable organizations will recognize that and promote you quickly. It may be a losing proposition over the short horizon, but if you look at it through the lens of your entire lifestyle, you will find yourself much richer in the end."
- ✓ "The hard skills that you have developed in the corporate sector are not only 110 percent transferable to the nonprofit sector, but they will be critical to your success."

Heather Rocker
Product Manager,
Georgia Center for Nonprofits, Atlanta, Georgia

Heather spent almost two years considering the move into the nonprofit sector from a position as a management consultant in an engineering firm. Prior to and during that time, Heather served as a board member for her local junior league, the America's Junior Miss Council, and the local chapter of her college alumni club. Heather read books about nonprofit jobs and conducted informational interviews with those already in the sector to determine whether she would need to go back to school for a nonprofit management degree or if her skills could translate without another degree. "After seven years in the world of consulting and through an extensive history of volunteer work," she explains, "I realized that I could effectively translate my technical and consulting experience to the nonprofit sector. And to be perfectly honest," she continues, "turning 30 does wonders for your life perspective and planning. It became a 'now or never' decision for me, and I'm thrilled that I took the leap."

To find her nonprofit job, Heather put the word out among her friends and colleagues whom she knew both through her business life and her nonprofit experience. Her main sources of job announcements were online job posting sites, and she found the best luck in searching those sites that were specifically targeted at nonprofit jobseekers. In hindsight, Heather would have gotten involved with local nonprofit organizations (such as Atlanta Nonprofit Professionals) during her job search to network effectively and learn more about working at nonprofits.

What challenges surprised Heather most in her job search?

"The challenge that I never saw coming," explains Heather, "was the one of convincing potential employers that I would actually accept a large pay decrease (counterintuitive to the job-hunting process)." In several searches, Heather would make it to the end of the process and then get turned down for fear that she would not stick with a job at a smaller salary in the long run. "There is definitely a pervasive theory in the nonprofit sector that those getting burned out in their current field turn to the nonprofits for a 'break,'" says Heather, who was called a "corporate refugee" on more than one occasion. She was shocked to find herself having to assure hiring managers that she understood and accepted the financial implications of this career transition and that this wasn't a sudden and purely "feel-good" decision.

In what ways did Heather prepare for the financial implications of this move?

"To be perfectly honest," says Heather, "the first task was to revisit the monthly household budget, realizing that raises would likely be more conservative and performance-based bonuses were a thing of the past." Heather researched average salaries for the job types she was pursuing and had a realistic idea of what salary would be offered. "I had to establish the bare minimum at which my husband and I could continue life as we knew it (but with a few more coupons in tow)."

Heather's Key Lessons Learned:

- ✓ "Don't assume that your job in the nonprofit sector will be without stress and pressures. One of the largest misconceptions about the nonprofit workplace is that the employees don't work as hard and everything is easier when, in fact, the opposite is true."
- ✓ "Know your ultimate goal in the sector and make sure your job is aligned accordingly. It is important to realize that keeping the books at the Boys and Girls Club headquarters is not at all the same as volunteering directly with the children."
- ✓ "Don't assume the nonprofit sector will be thrilled that someone from the corporate sector wants to transition to the nonprofit field. Anyone making the switch had better hone their answer to, 'Tell me why you want to come to the nonprofit sector?' and mean it!"

EPILOGUE

Throughout this book, you've read the stories of people who have made the transition from the corporate to the nonprofit sector. Some came by accident; others were more purposeful. All are thrilled with their decision, and most wished they had done it sooner.

Undoubtedly you picked up *Mission Driven* because you were curious about what working in the nonprofit sector would mean for you, personally, professionally, and financially. This book endeavored to help answer those questions and inspire you on your journey. Now you are ready—go follow your dream!

ABOUT THE AUTHOR

Laura Gassner Otting has spent the last 20 years working to strengthen organizations that weave our social and civic fabric. More than half of that time has been as the CEO of Nonprofit Professionals Advisory Group, a firm she founded to ensure that all nonprofits, regardless of their budget size and geographic footprint, had access to the most effective methods of securing that all important resource of talent. Over the past 11 years, she and her team have placed hundreds of leaders in nonprofits with budgets from $250,000 to $450,000,000, in the United States and around the world.

Prior to founding the Nonprofit Professionals Advisory Group in 2002, Laura helped build the start-up ExecSearches.com, a leading website for mid- to senior-level nonprofit job postings, and served as a vice president at Isaacson, Miller, one of the most highly respected nonprofit executive search firms in the country. Previously, Laura served as a presidential appointee for the White House Office of National Service and a program officer for the Corporation for National and Community Service where she was part of the team that created AmeriCorps, and as a member of the Clinton/Gore Transition Team and 1992 Election Team. Laura holds a Master of Arts in Political Management from the George Washington University and a Bachelor of Arts in Government from the University of Texas at Austin.

Laura serves on the boards of College Bound Dorchester, the Eli J. Segal Citizen Leadership Program at Brandeis University, and Newton Montessori School. She is a founding board member of SheGives, a philanthropy marketplace catalyzing support for a broad range of philanthropies around Boston. She has served as a member of the board of Camp Starfish and the Alumni Board of the Graduate School of Political Management at the George Washington University and as the founding board chair of both Strong Women, Strong Girls and the Boston Choral Ensemble. Laura is a curator for TedxBeaconStreet in Boston. Always up for a challenge, Laura completed the 2012, 2014

Boston and 2012 Chicago Marathons, in all cases, raising significant money for charities.

Laura is the author of *Change Your Career: Transitioning to the Nonprofit Sector* and is widely quoted for her expertise in mission-driven work in publications like *The New York Times*, *The Chronicle of Philanthropy* and *Money* magazine.

ACKNOWLEDGMENTS

The original manuscript of this book could not have been written without the help and support of so many friends, colleagues, and loved ones. Heaping mounds of gratitude go to Linda Babcock, Jack Goldsmith, Leslie Williams, Jameila Haddawi, Elizabeth Shreve, Jess Brooks, Amy Goldstein, Mark Miller, Caren and Jon Krumerman, Walter and Shelly Gassner, and Butch and Barbara Otting for helping me launch this project and for their sage wisdom, relentless support, and unending patience throughout. Special appreciation belongs to the editors at Kaplan Publishing who asked me to write that first publication; and to Makeba Greene and Jessica Cook, rock star researchers from Nonprofit Professionals Advisory Group, and the fine folks at Elevate, who helped me make it current once more. Mostly, though, I remain in debt to my children, Ben and Toby, who every day inspire me to make the world a better place, and to my husband, Jon, my wings and my safety net, who always remains my true north.

APPENDIX

This abridged list should give you a sense of the resources at your disposal as you make this transition into the nonprofit sector. A longer, more detailed list may be found at http://www.Nonprofitprofessionals.com.

Job Boards by Interest Area

General Nonprofit Job Websites
American Society of Association Executives –http://www.asaecenter.org/
Bridgestar – http://www.bridgestar.org
CEO Update – http://www.associationjobs.com
Chronicle of Philanthropy –http://philanthropy.com/jobs/
ExecSearches.com – http://www.execsearches.com
Guidestar – http://www.guidestar.org
Idealist – http://www.idealist.org
Nonprofit Oyster – http://www.Nonprofitoyster.com
Nonprofit Times – http://www.nptimes.com
Opportunity NOCs –http://www.opportunityNOCS.org

Academia, Teaching, and Higher Education
CASE – http://www.case.org
Chronicle of Higher Education –http://www.chronicle.com
Council for Special Education –http://www.specialedcareers.org/
Education Week – http://www.agentk–12.org
Higher Ed Jobs – http://www.higheredjobs.com

Animals and the Environment
American Zoo and Aquarium Association Positions –http://www.aza.org/JobListings/
Environmental Careers and Opportunities –http://www.ecojobs.com
EnviroJobs – EnviroJobs@yahoogroups.com
Environmental Jobs and Careers –http://www.ejobs.org/
Green Dream Jobs –http://www.sustainablebusiness.com/jobs/

Arts and Cultural
Arts Jobs – http://www.artjob.org
Arts Wire – http://www.artswire.org
Museum Jobs – http://www.museumjobs.org

Foundations and Philanthropy
Council on Foundations – http://www.cof.org
The Foundation Center with the Philanthropy News
Digest – http://www.fdncenter.org
On Philanthropy Job Bank –http://www.dotorgjobs.com/rt/dojhome
PNN Online – http://pnnonline.org/

Health and Medical
Health Careers Online –http://www.healthcareers–online.com
Health Career Web – http://www.healthcareerweb.com
Public Health Employment Connection –http://cfusion.sph.emory.edu/PHEC/phec.cfm

Appendix

International
    International Jobs – http://www.internationaljobs.org
    Overseas Jobs – http://www.overseasjobs.org
    U.S. Foreign Service – http://www.state.gov

Legal
    American Bar Associations – http://www.abanet.org
    Emplawyer – http://Emplawyer.net
    LawJobs – http://www.LawJobs.com

Lesbian, Gay, Bisexual and Transgender
    Diversity Working – http://www.diversityworking.com/career/Non_Profit/gay_lesbians.htm
    GLP Careers – http://www.glpcareers.com/
    ProGayJobs – http://www.progayjobs.com/Nonprofit.php
    Queer Jobs Listserv – queerjobs@yahoogroups.com

National and Community Service
    Community Career Center –http://www.Nonprofitjobs.org
    Idealist – http://www.idealist.org
    Lifetime of Service (AmeriCorps Alums) –http://www.lifetimeofservice.org/networking/
    VISTAnet – listserv@listserv.icors.org

Politics, Organizing and Government
    Careers in Government –http://www.careersingovernment.com
    National Organizers Alliance Job Bank –http://www.ultrabit.net/noa/jobbank.cfm
    Opportunities in Public Affairs – http://brubach.com
    Union Jobs Clearinghouse – http://www.unionjobs.com

Religious Organizations
    Christian Jobs Listserv –christian–jobs@yahoogroups.com
    Jewish Communal Jobs Clearinghouse –http://www.jewishjobs.com
    Ministry Connect – http://www.ministryconnect.org
    Work Ministry – http://www.workministry.com

Social Service
    Coalition for Human Needs –http://www.chn.org/jobs/index.html
    Jobs in Fair Housing – http://www.fairhousing.com
    Social Service Jobs – http://www.socialservice.com
    National Association of Social Workers JobLink –http://www.naswdc.org

Technology
    Contract Employment Weekly, Jobs Online – http://www.cjhunter.com
    Nonprofit Tech Jobs – http://groups.yahoo.com/group/Nonprofit_Tech_Jobs
    Dice.com – http://www.dice.com

Women
    Career Women – http://www.careerwomen.com/
    Feminist Majority Career Center –http://www.feminist.org
    Women's Information Network –http://www.winonline.org

Executive Search Firms Serving the Nonprofit Sector
    Auerbach Associates – http://www.auerbach–assc.com
    Commongood Careers – http://www.cgcareers.org
    Development Resource Group – http://www.drg.com

Appendix

Diversified Search – http://www.divsearch.com
Egmont and Associates –http://www.egmontassociates.com
Isaacson, Miller – http://www.imsearch.com
Kittleman & Associates, LLC – http://www.kittleman.com
Korn Ferry – http://www.kornferry.com
Lois Lindauer Searches – http://www.lllsearches.com
Morris & Berger – http://www.morrisberger.com
Nonprofit Professionals Advisory Group –http://www.Nonprofitprofessionals.com
Russell Reynolds Associates, Inc. –http://www.russellreynolds.com
Slesinger Management –http://www.slesingermanagement.com
Spencer Stuart – http://www.spencerstuart.com

Temp/Staffing Agencies Making Placements in Nonprofits

Accounting Management Solutions –http://www.amsolutions.net
Careers for Causes – http://www.placementpros.com/
First Source Staffing – http://fssny.com
Professionals for Nonprofits – http://www.nonprofitstaffi ng.com
Nonprofit Staffing Solutions – http://www.nonprofittemps.com/

Continued Reading

Books on Nonprofit Management

The Nonprofit Sector: A Research Handbook, by Walter W. Powell and Richard Steinberg, Yale
    University Press; 2nd Edition (November 1, 2006)
The Nature of the Nonprofit Sector by J. Steven Ott, Westview Press (October 1, 2000)
Good to Great and the Social Sector: A Monograph to Accompany Good to Great, Jim Collins,
    HarperCollins (November 30, 2005)
Love and Profit, James A. Autry, Harper Paperbacks; Reprint edition (September 1, 1992)
Leadership in Nonprofit Organizations: Lessons from the Third Sector, Barry Dym and Harry Hutson,
    Sage Publications, Inc (January 12, 2005)

Books with Inspirational Stories

The Cathedral Within, by Billy Shore, Random House Trade Paperbacks (November 1, 2001)
Leaving Microsoft to Change the World, by John Wood, Collins (August 29, 2006)
How to Change the World, by David Bornstein, Oxford University Press, USA (February 5, 2004)
Be the Change! Change the World. Change Yourself. Edited by Michelle Nunn, Hundreds of Heads
    Books (November 1, 2006)
Encore: How Baby Boomers Are Inventing the Next Stage of Work, by Marc Freedman, PublicAffairs
    (May 30, 2007)

Magazines, Periodicals, and Journals

Alliance Insight – http://www.allianceonline.org/insights.ipage
Chronicle of Higher Education – http://www.chronicle.com
Chronicle of Philanthropy – http://www.philanthropy.com
Contributions Magazine – http://www.contributionsmagazine.com
Exempt Magazine – http://www.exemptmagazine.com/
Fast Company – http://www.fastcompany.com
Generocity – http://www.generocitymag.com
Good Magazine – http://www.goodmagazine.com/
Nonprofit Quarterly – http://www.nonprofitquarterly.org/
Nonprofit Times – http://www.nptimes.com
Stanford Social Innovation Review –http://www.ssireview.org/

Appendix

E-Newsletters
    Bridgestar – http://www.bridgestar.org
    Case Foundation – http://www.casefoundation.org/about/contact/email–updates
    Charity Channel – http://charitychannel.com/enewsletters/ncr/index.asp
    Compass Point's Board Cafe – http://www.compasspoint.org/boardcafe/index.php
    Just Give – http://www.justgive.org/html/Nonprofits/npnewsletter.html
    Nonprofit About.com – http://Nonprofit.about.com/gi/pages/mmail.htm
    Nonprofit Legal Issues – http://www.Nonprofitissues.com/
    Nonprofit News Online – http://news.gilbert.org/
    Nonprofit Policy News – http://www.ncna.org/index.cfm?fuseaction=Page.viewPage&pageId=696
    Nonprofit Professionals Advisory Group –http://www.Nonprofitprofessionals.com
    Omidyar Network – http://www.omidyar.net/home/
    Skoll Foundation – http://www.skollfoundation.org/

Helpful Websites for Additional Research
    Charity Navigator – http://www.charitynavigator.org
    Guidestar – http://www.guidestar.org
    National Center for Charitable Statistics – http://nccs.urban.org
    Network for Good – http://www.networkforgood.org
    The Nonprofit FAQs – http://www.nonprofits.org

Educational Resources:
Degrees or Concentrations in Nonprofit

Graduate Programs (Graduate Degrees)
The following schools offer programs where you can earn your Master of Arts (MA), Master of Business Administration (MBA), Master of Nonprofit Administration, (MNA), Master of Public Administration (MPA), Master of Public Policy (MPP), Master of Science (MS), or Doctor of Philosophy (PhD) in nonprofit management.

Alabama
    Auburn University at Montgomery, MPA with Concentration in Nonprofit

Arizona
    Arizona State University, MPA in Nonprofit Management
    University of Arizona, MPA in Nonprofits and Government

California
    University of San Francisco, MNA
    University of California at Los Angeles, MPP in Nonprofit Policy
    San Francisco State University, MPA in Nonprofit Administration
    University of San Diego, MA in Nonprofit Leadership and Management Studies
    University of Southern California, MPA and MPP with Concentrations in Nonprofit Management

Colorado
    Regis University, MNA
    University of Colorado at Denver, MPA, Doctor of Philosophy in Public Administration

Connecticut
    University of Connecticut, MPA with Concentration in Nonprofit Management
    Yale University, MBA with Concentration in Nonprofit Management

Appendix

District of Columbia
Georgetown University, MPA in Nonprofit Policy and Leadership
The George Washington University, MPA and MPP with Concentrations in Nonprofit Management

Delaware
University of Delaware, MA and MPA with Concentrations in Community Development and
    Nonprofit Leadership

Florida
Florida Atlantic University, MNA

Georgia
Georgia State University, MPA in Nonprofit Studies, MS in Urban Policy Studies in Nonprofit
    Studies
Kennesaw State University, MPA in Community Services/Nonprofit Administration
University of Georgia, MA in Nonprofit Organizations

Iowa
University of Northern Iowa, MA in Philanthropy and Nonprofit Development, MPP in Nonprofits

Illinois
DePaul University, MS in Public Service Management with Concentrations in Association and
    Management, MS in Public Service Management in Fundraising and Philanthropy, MS in Public
    Service Management in Nonprofit Administration
Northwestern University, Master of Nonprofit Management
Southern Illinois University at Edwardsville, MPA
Illinois Institute of Technology, MPA in Nonprofit Management

Indiana
Indiana University at Bloomington, MPA and PhD with Concentrations in Nonprofit Management
Indiana University, Center on Philanthropy, MA in Philanthropic Studies, MPA in Nonprofit
    Management, PhD in Philanthropic Studies
Indiana University-Purdue University at Indianapolis, MPA in Nonprofit Management
University of Notre Dame, MS in Nonprofit Leadership

Louisiana
Louisiana State University at Shreveport, MS in Human Services Administration

Maine
Clark University, MPA in Nonprofit Administration

Maryland
College of Notre Dame of Maryland, MA in Nonprofit Management
Johns Hopkins University, MA in Policy Studies in Nonprofit Sector
University of Maryland, University College, MA in Management in Nonprofit Management

Massachusetts
Harvard University, MPP, MPA, PhD in Public Policy / Public Administration
Lesley College, MBA in Not-for-Profit Management
Tufts University, MA in Nonprofit Organizations
Worcester State College, MS in Nonprofit Management

155

Appendix

Michigan
Oakland University, MPA in Nonprofit Organization and Management
University of Michigan, MSW, MPA, MPP with Concentrations in Nonprofit Management
Wayne State University, Master of Interdisciplinary Studies in Nonprofit Sectors
Western Michigan University, MPA in Nonprofit Management and Leadership

Minnesota
St. Cloud State University, MS in Public and Nonprofit Institutions
University of Minnesota, Humphrey Institute, Master of Public Affairs in Nonprofits, Master of
    Management in Nonprofits

Missouri
University of Missouri at Kansas City, MPA in Nonprofit Management, Doctor of Philosophy in
    Public
Administration in Nonprofit Management
University of Missouri at St. Louis, MPP in Nonprofit Management and Leadership

North Carolina
High Point University, MPA in Nonprofit Organizations
University of North Carolina at Greensboro, Master of Public Affairs in Nonprofit Management

Nebraska
University of Nebraska at Omaha, MPA in Nonprofit, Doctor of Philosophy in Public Administration
    in Nonprofit

New Jersey
Seton Hall University, MPA in Nonprofit Management
Kean University, MPA in Nonprofit Management

New York
CUNY - Baruch College, MPA in Nonprofit Administration
Long Island University, MPA in Not-for-Profit Management
New School University, MS in Nonprofit Management
New York University - Wagner Graduate School, MPA and Doctor of Philosophy with Specializations
    in Public and Nonprofit Management and Policy,
Management of International Public Service Organizations, and Nonprofit and NGOs

Ohio
Case Western Reserve University, MNA, Executive Doctor of Management
Cleveland State University, MA in Nonprofit Management, Doctor of Philosophy in Nonprofit
    Management
Kent State University, MBA in Nonprofit Management, MPA in Nonprofit Management
Ohio State University, Master of Social Work in Social Administration Practice
The Union Institute, MA in Nonprofit Management, PhD in Nonprofit Management

Oregon
Portland State University - Division of Public Administration, MPA in Nonprofit, Doctor of
    Philosophy in Public Administration and Policy in Nonprofit
University of Oregon, Master of Community & Regional Planning, MPA, Graduate Certificate in
    Not-for-Profit Management

Appendix

Pennsylvania

Eastern University, MS in Nonprofit Management

Indiana University of Pennsylvania, Mater of Arts in Sociology in Administration & Evaluation and Human Services Administration, Doctor of Philosophy in Administration and Leadership Studies in Administration & Evaluation and Human Services Administration

Widener University, MPA in Nonprofit Administration

South Carolina

College of Charleston, MPA in Nonprofit Administration

South Dakota

University of South Dakota, MPA in Nonprofit Administration

Tennessee

University of Memphis, MPA in Nonprofit Administration

University of Tennessee, Chattanooga, MPA in Nonprofit Management

Texas

University of Houston – Victoria, MA in Interdisciplinary Studies in Nonprofit Leadership

University of Texas at Austin, Lyndon B. Johnson School of Public Affairs, MPA, PhD in Public Policy

University of Dallas, MBA in Nonprofit Management, MS in Management in Nonprofit Management

Virginia

George Mason University, MPA in Nonprofit Management

Virginia Commonwealth University, MPA in Nonprofit Management

Vermont

School for International Training, Program in Intercultural Service, Leadership, and Management (PIM) in Mission Driven Organizations

Washington

Seattle University, Executive Master of Not-For-Profit Leadership, MPA in Nonprofit Leadership

Wisconsin

University of Wisconsin – Milwaukee, MA, MBA, MPA in Nonprofit Management

Certificate Programs (Graduate Programs)

Alabama

Auburn University at Montgomery, Nonprofit Management and Leadership Certificate

University of Alabama at Birmingham, Graduate Certificate in Nonprofit Management

Arkansas

University of Arkansas at Little Rock, Graduate Certificate in Nonprofit Management

California

California State University – Hayward, Nonprofit Management Certificate

University of San Diego, Certificate in Nonprofit Leadership & Management

Calstate East Bay, Certificate in Nonprofit Management

Colorado

University of Colorado at Colorado Springs, Certificate in Nonprofit Management

Appendix

Connecticut
University of Connecticut, Graduate Certificate in Nonprofit Management

District of Columbia
The George Washington University, Graduate Certificate in Nonprofit Management

Florida
Florida Atlantic University, Nonprofit Management Executive Certificate

Georgia
Georgia State University, Graduate Certificate in Nonprofit Management
University of Georgia, Graduate Certificate in Nonprofit Organizations

Illinois
DePaul University, Administrative Foundations Certificate, Nonprofit Leadership Certificate
Southern Illinois University at Edwardsville, Non-Profit Management Certificate
Illinois Institute of Technology, Certificate in Nonprofit Management
Loyola University Chicago, Certificate of Advanced Study in Philanthropy
Saint Xavier University, Certificate in Public and Non-Profit Management

Indiana
Indiana University – Bloomington, Nonprofit Management Certificate
Indiana University, Center on Philanthropy, Philanthropic Studies Certificate, Nonprofit Management Certificate
Purdue University, Certificate in Nonprofit Management
Perdue University North Central, Certificate in Nonprofit Management

Maryland
College of Notre Dame of Maryland, Certificate in Leadership of Nonprofit Organizations
Johns Hopkins University, Certificate in Nonprofit Studies
University of Maryland, University College, Nonprofit Financial Management Certificate

Massachusetts
Tufts University, Management of Community
Organizations Certificate

Michigan
Oakland University, Post-Master's Certificate in Nonprofit Organization & Management
University of Michigan, Certificate in Nonprofit Management in Development
Ferris State University, Philanthropic Studies Certificate
Grand Valley State University, Graduate Certificate in Nonprofit Leadership
Lawrence Technological University, Graduate Certificate in Nonprofit Management and Leadership
Wayne State University, Master of Interdisciplinary Studies in Nonprofit Sectors
Western Michigan University, Nonprofit Leadership Certificate

Minnesota
University of Minnesota, Humphrey Institute, Nonprofit Management Certificate

Missouri
University of Missouri at Kansas City, Fund Raising Certificate
University of Missouri at St. Louis, Nonprofit Management and Leadership Certificate

Appendix

New Jersey
Seton Hall University, Certificate in Nonprofit Organization Management
Rutgers University – Newark, Certificate in Nonprofit Management

New York
Roberts Wesleyan College, Certificate in Nonprofit Leadership
C.W. Post College, Nonprofit Management Advanced Certificate
SUNY College at Brockport, Certificate in Nonprofit Management

Nevada
University of Nevada, Certificate in Nonprofit Management

North Carolina
North Carolina State University, Graduate Certificate in Nonprofit Management
University of North Carolina – Greensboro, Nonprofit Management Certificate
University of North Carolina at Chapel Hill, Nonprofit Leadership Certificate
University of North Carolina at Chapel Hill, Social Work, Nonprofit Leadership Certificate

Ohio
Case Western Reserve University, Certificate in Nonprofit Management
Cleveland State University, Certificate in Nonprofit Management
University of Akron, Certificate in Nonprofit Management

Oregon
Portland State University - Division of Public Administration, Nonprofit Management Certificate, Nonprofit Development Certificate, Nonprofit Financial Management Certificate, Volunteer Management Certificate
University of Oregon, Graduate Certificate in Not-for-Profit Management

Pennsylvania
University of Pennsylvania, Certificate in Nonprofit Administration
University of Pittsburgh, Nonprofit Management Certificate
Widener University, Certificate of Advanced Graduate Studies in Nonprofit Management

Rhode Island
Rhode Island College, Certificate in Nonprofit Studies

Tennessee
University of Tennessee, Chattanooga, Certificate in Nonprofit Management

Texas
University of Dallas, Certificate for Not-for-Profit Management
University of North Texas, Graduate Academic
Certificate in Volunteer and Community Resource Management

Virginia
George Mason University, Certificate in Nonprofit Management, Certificate in Association Management
Virginia Commonwealth University, Graduate Certificate in Nonprofit Management
Virginia Tech, Nonprofit and Nongovernmental Organization Management Certificate

Washington
University of Washington, Nonprofit Management Certificate

Appendix

West Virginia

West Virginia University, Nonprofit Management Certificate

Wisconsin

University of Wisconsin – Milwaukee, Graduate Certificate in Nonprofit Management

Continuing Education (CEU)

Arizona

Arizona State University, Nonprofit Management

California

California State University at Hayward, Non-Profit Management

California State University at Fresno, Nonprofit Leadership and Management

California State University, Fullerton, Leadership for Public and Nonprofit Service

San Jose State University, Nonprofit Management

University of California at Irvine, Fundraising

University of San Francisco, Executive Nonprofit Management, Development Director

Florida

University of South Florida, Nonprofit Management

Indiana

Indiana University – Bloomington, Nonprofit Management

Indiana University, Center on Philanthropy, Fundraising Management

Maryland

Goucher College, Nonprofit Management

Michigan

Michigan State University, Excellence in Nonprofit Leadership & Management

Oakland University, Nonprofit Management

Minnesota

University of St. Thomas - Center for Nonprofit Management, Mini-MBA for Nonprofit Organizations

Missouri

University of Missouri at Kansas City, Fund Raising Management

Nebraska

University of Nebraska at Omaha, Fundraising Management

New York

New York University - School of Continuing & Professional Studies, Fundraising

The Union Institute, Certified Volunteer Manager

Oregon

Portland State University - Division of Public Administration, Nonprofit Management, Nonprofit Development, Nonprofit Financial Management, Volunteer Management

Pennsylvania

Bryn Mawr College, Executive Leadership

Appendix

Marywood University, Program in Non-Profit Management

Texas

University of Texas at Austin - Thompson Conference Center, Management of Nonprofit Organizations

Virginia

University of Richmond, Philanthropy

Washington

Washington State University, Volunteer Management

West Virginia

West Virginia University, Nonprofit Management

Wisconsin

University of Wisconsin at Milwaukee, Professional Nonprofit Management
University of Wisconsin at Superior, Nonprofit Administration

Online

California State University, Long Beach, MPA
Capella University, MS, Ph.D. in Human Services/ Management of Nonprofit
George Mason University, MPA, Certificate in Nonprofit Management, Certificate in Association Management
Indiana University-Purdue University-Indianapolis, Certificate in Nonprofit Management
Regis University, Master of Nonprofit Management
University of Colorado at Denver, MPA with Concentration in Nonprofit Organization Management
University of Illinois at Chicago, Certificate for Nonprofit Management, School of Public and Environmental Affairs (SPEA), Nonprofit Management Certificate
University of Maryland, Not-for-Profit Financial Management Graduate Certificate
University of San Francisco, Development Director Certificate
Walden University, MBA, MPA, Ph.D., Nonprofit Management and Leadership

INDEX

Index

Index

Index

The companion handbook for
Mission Driven: Moving from Profit to Purpose

Filled with case studies, exercises, and examples, *The Mission Driven Handbook* is a must-have resource that provides the job seeker with the tools and directions necessary to launch a career in the nonprofit sector.

Grab Your Copy Wherever Fine Books Are Sold

Find resources and news about *Mission Driven* and *The Mission Driven Handbook* at:

www.bemissiondriven.com